The Place Names
of the
White Mountains

The Flume, from *Oakes*.

The
Place Names
of the
White Mountains

History and Origins
by Robert and Mary Hixon

DOWN EAST BOOKS

With Love and hope, we dedicate this book
to our daughter, Megan Mae

INTRODUCTION

T HIS BOOK is about the names, the places, and ultimately the people of the White Mountains. It is an attempt to discover and present in a clear and interesting manner the meanings and origins of the names of the mountains, lakes, rivers, towns, villages, and other geographical features of the northern third of New Hampshire comprising the White Mountains region.

The region is vast. Beginning north of Lake Winnipesaukee, it extends north over a hundred miles to the Canadian border, and it includes within its boundaries several major mountain ranges and the headwaters and drainage basins of four major rivers. Defining the region is difficult. For the purposes of this book, we have defined the White Mountains to include all the area north of and including the following towns: Piermont, Warren, Ellsworth, Campton, Thornton, Waterville Valley, Albany, and Conway. This is a delineation used by other writers and by mapmakers and planners within New Hampshire. And although some towns south of this boundary certainly share in the characteristics and ambience of the White Mountains, we felt they were more properly a part of what is called the Lakes Region. The White Mountains are bounded on the west by the Connecticut River, which is also the boundary between New Hampshire and Vermont. And on the east the region is bounded by the Maine border, although we have attempted to include place names from Maine where the mountains themselves have extended into that state.

Because of the great size of this region, and because many place names are duplicated within it — there are three Sugarloaf Mts. — we have attempted to list with our entries the sub-regions in which the names are located. This has been very difficult, because river basins overlap mountain ranges, and both are often ignored by political delineations. To resolve this, and to make the book easier to use, we have followed the system of regional subdivision used by the Appalachian Mountain Club (AMC) in its guidebooks. For example, if a name is listed as being in the Carter-Moriah Range, the place is located in the Carter-Moriah Range section of the AMC guides. The only exception is along the Connecticut River where we have included names from areas not covered by the AMC guides. For this area we have created a special subdivision called the Connecticut Region.

In any study of the place names of a region, the places come first. The broad topographical features of a region, its mountains and watersheds, both precede and endure after the assigning of names to them. Thus the places of a region are often a palimpsest upon which many peoples have written. In the White Mountains, literally thousands of places exist, ranging in size and significance from major mountain ranges to inconspicuous hillocks, from major rivers to tiny rivulets. And whether a place has a name depends solely upon whether people have felt the need to give it one, for place names are nothing more or less than a means of identification. In the vast wilderness north of the Presidential Range, a region little touched by human activity or penetration, dozens of mountains and scores of streams exist undistinguished by names. But in the central portion of the White Mountains, which has been more intensively explored and traveled, virtually all the mountain prominences and water bodies have been named.

In this book we have been deliberately arbitrary in selecting among the thousands of names that exist in the White Mountains which ones we wanted to include. Clearly, the names of the major geographical features were to be included, even where origins and meanings of the names are obvious and self-explanatory, as with Twin Mt. We have sought, for example, to include an entry for each peak over 3,500 feet. We have also attempted to include an entry for each of the more important geopolitical places, such as towns, villages, and settlements.

But this book is about names as much as it is about places. And some names are included simply because they are fascinating, or because they carry with them an interesting story, even though the place they identify has little familiarity or significance. Chickwolnepy Brook in the Mahoosuc Range, for example, has little to distinguish it — except its name. And northeast of the village of Lancaster is a rural district similar to many others in the White Mountains except that it is known as Lost Nation, yet who could resist curiosity about this name?

And ultimately, this book is about the people of the White Mountains, for they gave the names. Place names, paradoxically, are among the most enduring and the most ephemeral of human artifacts. Of the Indian peoples who inhabited the White Mountains for thousands of years little has survived in our general consciousness — except the names they gave to places. Yet the Indian place names that have not survived have vanished utterly, forever beyond recall.

Place names are also among the most revealing of human artifacts; study how the names of a region came to be and you will have insight into the lives and values of the peoples that lived and traveled in that region. Place names preserve a wide range of human experience. In the White Mountains, the names were given by explorers, settlers, legislators, farmers, fishermen, hunters, organizations, local officials, and storytellers. The names recall Presidents, wandering tinkers, English noblemen, obscure settlers, famous statesmen, eccentric hermits, hunters, hikers, scientists, soldiers, Indian chiefs, Indian squaws, merchants, roadbuilders, innkeepers, poets, artists, and even mythical figures. Some names, such as Spruce Mt., are prosaically descriptive; others, such as Diana's Baths, are poetic and fanciful. The names were given in honor, in anger, and in humor.

The Indians were the first name-givers in the White Mountains. Of their history and culture in the region little remains. By 1800 most of them had vanished from New Hampshire, their numbers decimated by disease and warfare and their lands occupied by increasing numbers of white settlers. Linguistic studies of the Abenaki-speaking survivors of these peoples have been undertaken by Father Rales, Rev. John Aubrey, and Prof. John C. Huden, and their work provides valuable insights into how the Indians referred to places in the White Mountains. For example, it becomes clear that in the White Mountains as elsewhere Indian place names tend to be descriptive: the name Ammonoosuc translates to mean "fish-place," and the name Pemigewasset means "swift current." These names were adopted by white settlers often with an imperfect understanding of their meanings and even more often with an imperfect perception of their pronunciations. For example, written records contain no less than fifty variant spellings of the name Winnipesaukee.

Many place names in the White Mountains honor Indian personages: Chocorua, Paugus, Kancamagus, Passaconaway, Weetamoo, Mollocket, and others. But these names were all assigned by whites, and usually long after the Indians they honored had departed. They are more the stuff of legend than of history.

The first white man to climb Mt. Washington was Darby Field, who made his ascent in 1642. Indian danger and remoteness kept most whites away from the White Mountains for about a hundred years until 1761 when Gov. Benning Wentworth, the first royal governor of New Hampshire, began making extensive grants of land, often to veterans of the French and Indian Wars, so that settlers might develop the new territories. Gov. Benning Wentworth was succeeded in 1767 by his nephew, John Wentworth, who was governor until 1775, and together the Wentworth governors granted and named most of the towns in the White Mountains. Almost invariably the names they assigned honored English business and political associates of the Wentworths. Many of these names were subsequently changed, especially when the lands they designated were not settled; other names survive, in towns such as Bath, Colebrook, Conway, Errol, Landaff, Northumberland, and Stewartstown. Many persons selected by the Wentworths to be so honored were influential Englishmen who advocated mild treatment of the American colonies.

When the Revoluntionary War broke out, the Wentworths departed. When a new nation emerged from the conflict, so did a new era of naming in the White Mountains; Americans instead of Englishmen were honored. Scientific expeditions, such as the one led by Dr. Jeremy Belknap in 1784, began entering the White Mountains, and many place names honor early explorers: Manasseh Cutler, Philip Carrigain, Jacob Bigelow, Francis Boott, Lemuel Shaw, Edward Tuckerman, and others. Many early explorers were botanists, and rarely has the exploration and naming of geographical features owed so much to the search for botanical features.

But the names these explorers themselves bestowed in the White Mountains were often to honor American patriots. Mt. Washington was named during this period, as well as most of the other peaks on the Presidential Range. The town of Columbia on the upper Connecticut River received its name during the patriotic enthusiasm preceding the War of 1812. Signers of the Declaration of Independence were honored by place names in the White Mountains, as were other prominent figures of the Revolutionary era.

But throughout this period, while the formal commemorative names were being given, other less formal but no less important or enduring names were evolving. Settlers of the White Mountains needed names to identify brooks, mountains, fords, clearings, trails, notches, and so forth; very often names were not assigned but merely sprang up. A pond where a man named Ladd settled became known as Ladd Pond; a path following an open artificial waterway became known as Aqueduct Path; a settlement that grew up around a sawmill built by a man named Kidder became known as Kidderville; a tract of land granted to a man named Martin was known as Martin's Grant; the notch where Daniel Pinkham tried to build a road was called Pinkham Notch; and the pond where a man named Diamond shot a moose took the name Diamond Pond.

Local people liked to talk about the place names in their vicinity, and legends and tall tales grew up around them. In this book we have frequently and unashamedly used phrases such as "according to tradition" and "legend says." There is no way of verifying whether these legends are true, or whether they are not. Very often they are the only information that exists regarding a place name. And even when it is very likely that a legend is indeed apocryphal, we have still included it, because such legends are part of the character and color of a place. No one today sincerely believes, as the Indians did, that evil spirits reside on Mt. Washington, but knowing that once people did believe they lived there adds to our appreciation of the mountain.

By the mid-1800's a new group of people were coming to the White Mountains, and increasingly hotels, railroads, and paths were built to accommodate them. They were writers and artists, and while they were still interested in exploration, they were also interested in recreation and communion with nature. A product of the romantic and transcendentalist movements in American thought, their writings and the names they bestowed reflect a deep appreciation of the beauty of the White Mountains. Nathaniel Hawthorne wrote his famous short story about the Old Man of the Mountain; the Rev. Thomas Starr King popularized the region with his highly descriptive writings; a school of landscape artists devoted themselves to portraying the rugged beauty of the mountains; and persons such as Henry David Thoreau, Daniel Webster, and John Greenleaf Whittier visited the area. It was during this period that appeared names such as Arethusa Falls, Diana's Baths, Mt. Avalon, Cathedral Ledge, and those given to honor legendary Indian figures.

The latter part of the nineteenth century was the last great period of naming in the White Mountains, with two important events occurring in 1876. In that year New Hampshire State Geologist Charles H. Hitchcock published his map of the White Mountains, and also in that year the Appalachian Mountain Club was born.

Few persons have known as much about the history and geography of the White Mountains as Charles H. Hitchcock. For forty years he was a professor of geology at Dartmouth College, and in 1868 he was appointed State Geologist of New Hampshire, where he undertook a geological survey of the state. He was a frequent and thorough explorer of the White Mountains, and many of its features were discovered by him and his associates. He also named many places, and literally dozens of features appear for the first time on the map he published in 1876.

And on Jan. 1, 1876, Prof. E. Charles Pickering mailed cards of invitation to fifty persons "interested in mountain exploration," and thus the Appalachian Mountain Club was conceived. The club was formally organized soon thereafter, and during the years since then the AMC has had a continuing, intimate, and constructive relationship with the White Mountains. Committees were formed on trail construction and maintenance, and AMC officers and members such as J. Rayner Edmands, William G. Nowell, and others were largely responsible for the system of trails and huts presently existing in the White Mountains. These AMC members named many of the trails they built, and in return many trails and features were named for them.

The AMC also set up a Committee on Nomenclature to study mountain names and to arbitrate disputes. For example, this committee ruled that Mt. Clinton, which had been renamed Mt. Pierce by the New Hampshire Legislature, should retain its original name on AMC maps. And this committee also decided against changing the name of a mountain in the town of Northumberland from Cape Horn to Mt. Lyon, as had been proposed. Many of this committee's decisions have since been ratified by time and usage; a few are still contested.

And it should be realized that disputes regarding place names in the White Mountains have been common. The most famous example is the name of the mountain east of Conway now known as Kearsarge North but formerly known simply as Kearsarge, although some mapmakers labeled the mountain Pequawket. Another Mt. Kearsarge existed in the town of Warner, and for years a controversy smoldered as to which peak should bear that name. Local people in Conway had long called their mountain Kearsarge, and with vehemence and indignation they insisted on their right to continue doing so. Finally a compromise solution was reached whereby the northern peak would be called Kearsarge North.

We have encountered many such conflicts in preparing this book. It would have been impossible to include separate entries for all the names of all the features we have listed, so we have based our entries on the names as given in the AMC guides and on maps of the New Hampshire Department of Highways. Where two "official" names exist, as with Mt. Clinton-Pierce and Mt. Cannon-Profile, we have prepared entries under both names. But under each entry we have also sought to include as many local names and variants as we could find, and we made no attempt either to validate or invalidate them.

Very often we have encountered conflicts in our sources regarding the origins of names. Where possible we have sought to resolve the conflict. For example, some sources give the origin of the name Pilot Mt. as the name of a dog belonging to a hermit who lived nearby. It's an interesting tale, and we have mentioned it, but the presence of the name Land Pilot Hills on early maps that would likely pre-date the hermit and his dog suggest another origin for the name.

Because of conflicts such as the one mentioned above, it often was important to know when a name first appeared either on a map or in print; although these early works did not necessarily explain the origin of a name, they often were useful in verifying other information. Works that provided important first references included: Samuel Holland's *A Topographical Map of the State of New Hampshire*, 1784; Jeremy Belknap's *History of New Hampshire*, 1784—1792, and his "A Map of New Hampshire," 1791; Philip Carrigain's *Map of New Hampshire*, 1816; the diary of Lucy Crawford, wife of Ethan Allen Crawford; George P. Bond's *A Map of the White Mountains*, 1853; Thomas Starr King's *The White Hills*, 1859; and Charles H. Hitchcock's "Map of New Hampshire," 1878. Town charter maps, many of which are located in the New Hampshire State Library, often provided first mention of local names.

But many conflicts have defied resolution — the name Bowman Mt. is an example — and in these instances we have included all relevant explanations and theories without attempting to arbitrate among them.

The origins and meanings of some place names have eluded us

altogether. Records and recollections regarding these names are either incomplete or nonexistent. The study of place names is a continuing search, and we hope readers who can supply information about names not in this book or additional information about names we have included will contact us.

These, then, are the place names of the White Mountains. Like the mountains themselves, they are subject in their details to continuing change and modification, yet in their general outlines they preserve a record of the history of the region. They are also interesting and fun, and we like to think of the place names of a region as a group of old-timers and characters from history sitting around telling stories and recounting reminiscences about their past. We have enjoyed preparing this book, and we hope you enjoy reading it.

Robert and Mary Hixson

ACKNOWLEDGEMENTS

P REPARATION of a book such as this clearly would have been impossible without the kind cooperation of the many persons who assisted us in answering questions, and to these persons we are sincerely grateful. But we feel we owe a special debt of gratitude to the entire staff of the Weeks Memorial Library in Lancaster for their assistance, patience, and trust. Also deserving special appreciation are Bill and Iris Baird of Lancaster, Joe and Virginia Richardson of Lancaster, Edna Whyte of Lancaster, Glenn J. Ackroyd of Gorham, Elaine D. Adjutant of Ossipee, Barbara Berry of Wolfeboro Falls, Samuel I. Bowditch of Tucson, Arizona, and Chocorua, George E. Brixton of Wolfeboro, Marjorie E. Broad of Campton, Mrs. C. L. Dodge of Lisbon, Alfred L. Dowden of Ossipee, Donald A. Lapham of Wolfeboro, James Mykland of Center Sandwich, Richard Roberts of Woodstock, Connecticut, Chilton Thomson of Cleveland, Ohio, and Frederic L. Steele of the White Mountain School in Littleton.

And finally, we owe a debt of gratitude to Peter E. Randall of Hampton, whose knowledge of the White Mountains and whose reading of our manuscript yielded many needed and important recommendations, and to Walter Wright, Curator of Rare Books, Baker Library, Dartmouth College, who also read the manuscript and who also provided many valuable suggestions.

A

Mt. Adams and the Mt. Washington Carriage Road, from *Bryant*.

A

Abenaki, Mt.   2,653 feet   *North Country*

The Abenaki Indians once inhabited most of New Hampshire, but they retreated northward before the advance of white settlers. The name "Abenaki" is thought to be derived from *Wan-ban-auke*, which to Indians of other tribes meant "the people living in the land of the Northern Lights *(Wan-ban-ben)*." The name is also thought to refer to people living in the "dawn-land," or more simply "easterners." The peak forming the north flank of Dixville Notch preserves the memory of these people.

A

Acteon Ridge   *Waterville Valley*

Running from Bald Knob to Jennings Peak, this ridge recalls the twilight days of the Pemigewasset Indians. They had a village at Franklin, and it is said that their last *sachem*, or chief, was named Acteon. This ridge was named for him by Prof. C. E. Fay of Tufts College.

Adams, Mt.   5,798 feet   *Northern Peaks*

Mt. Adams, the second highest peak in New England, is actually three summits, all closely related; and each is named for an American patriot named Adams, two of whom are also related. The highest summit, 5,798 feet, was christened Mt. John Adams on July 31, 1820, by the Weeks-Brackett naming party from nearby Lancaster, New Hampshire, (see Presidential Range).

The northernmost of the three peaks is also named for a President, also named Adams, and also named John. In 1857 Rev. Thomas Starr

King named this 5,470-foot summit in honor of the nation's sixth President, John Quincy Adams, son of President Adams.

And finally, in 1876, some Appalachian Mountain Club members jokingly referred to the most westerly peak as Sam Adams — and the name stuck. Today this 5,585-foot summit honors the American pamphleteer and advocate of independence, Samuel Adams.

Agassiz Basin   *Moosilauke Region*

On Moosilauke Brook, near N.H. Rte. 112 in Woodstock, is an interesting series of potholes named, as was Mt. Agassiz, for the great Swiss naturalist Jean Louis Rudolph Agassiz.

Agassiz, Mt.   2,378 feet   *Cannon-Kinsman*

Formerly known both as Peaked Mt. and Pickett Hill, this peak near Bethlehem was renamed in 1876 by New Hampshire State Geologist Charles H. Hitchcock to honor Jean Louis Rudolph Agassiz, the great Swiss explorer and naturalist who visited the White Mountains in 1846 and again in 1870.

Air Line Trail   *Northern Peaks*

E. B. Cook and L. M. Watson in 1882 cut this path leading from what is now the Appalachia Trailhead on U.S. Rte. 2 to Mt. Adams, and its name is probably derived from their decision to follow a ridge line. All previous trails had followed valleys.

Akers Pond   *North Country*

Northwest of the village of Errol is this pond, named for the Akers family who once owned much of the pond's shoreline.

Albany, Town   *Chocorua Region*

West of Conway is the town of Albany, whose boundaries include the peaks of Chocorua, Paugus, Three Sisters, Pequawket, and South Moat. Albany was originally chartered as Burton in 1766, most likely in honor of General Jonathan Burton of Wilton, New Hampshire, but in 1833 it was renamed Albany, and sources suggest this was because 1833 was the year the railroad from New York City to Albany, New York, was chartered.

Alpine Garden   *Mt. Washington*

It's not known exactly when or by whom this meadow between the Tuckerman Ravine Trail and the Mt. Washington Auto Road was named, but it was called the Alpine Garden by Moses F. Sweetser in his 1876 White Mountains guide. The reason for the name is clear: the meadow, in proper season, is dappled with alpine wildflowers blooming as in a garden. Some of the diminutive arctic plants growing in the tundra there are found nowhere else in New England.

Ames, Mt.   2,270 feet   *Chatham Region*

Fisher Ames (1756—1808) was an American statesman, and from him comes the name of this peak near Chatham. Ames's cousin, Dr. Joshua Fisher, participated in Dr. Jeremy Belknap's expedition to the White Mountains in 1784.

Ammonoosuc Ravine   *Mt. Washington*

One of the most direct routes to the upper slopes of the Presidential Range is up this steep ravine connecting the Cog Railroad Base Station with the Lakes of the Clouds. Its name is thought to have originated with Moses F. Sweetser, who named the ravine for the river that created it. Lucy Crawford, in her diary, tells the story of two travelers from Boston who in 1823 named the ravine "Escape Glen." As they made their way down it from Lakes of the Clouds, one of them nearly perished when a stump to which he was clinging broke off and sent him falling fifty feet.

Ammonoosuc Rivers

Three rivers in the White Mountains — the Upper Ammonoosuc, the Ammonoosuc further south, and the Wild Ammonoosuc further south still — all derive their names from an Abenaki Indian word meaning "fish-place." The Abenaki root word is variously cited as *namaos-auke, ompompanusuck,* and *namaos-coo-auke,* but their meanings are roughly the same. *Namos* meant "fish," and *-auke* was a

A

Ammonoosuc Falls, from *King*.

suffix meaning "place." Because of this, the names of the Ammonoosuc rivers in the White Mountains and the Amoskeag River in central New Hampshire have a common origin.

Anderson, Mt.   3,722 feet   *Pemigewasset-Carrigain*

Located northeast of Carrigain Notch, this peak was named by New Hampshire State Geologist Charles H. Hitchcock in 1876 for John E. Anderson of Portland, Maine. Mr. Anderson was chief engineer of the Portland and Ogdensburg Railroad, which in 1875 had opened a line through Crawford Notch.

Androscoggin River

This name is derived from an Abenaki word meaning "fish-curing place." The Indians are reported to have called this river *Amariscoggin*, a name having the same meaning.

Appalachia   *Northern Peaks*

An important trailhead on U. S. Rte. 2 in Randolph, Appalachia received its name when it was a railroad station (1896—1941). The station was intended primarily for guests of the Ravine House, but it also served as a meeting place for hikers. According to tradition, the name was born one Sunday afternoon soon after the station was opened when some boys on a Sunday school picnic from Berlin stole some green apples from the trees at the Ravine House. That night the boys sat in the station holding their stomachs in pain as they awaited transportation home. The sight so amused the guests of the Ravine House that, acting in committee, they unanimously approved naming the new train station "Apple-ache-ia." It was only natural that in time this would be elided to become Appalachia.

Appalachian Mountains

A

The name of one of North America's great mountain ranges, stretching from Georgia to Maine, originated at a poor Indian village in Florida. When the Spanish explorer Navarez launched an expedition into Florida seeking cities of gold, he found instead only a very ordinary Indian village called Apalchen. The Spaniards remembered this name, and eventually it was used on maps to designate the vague and mountainous interior. Still later, changed in spelling and pronunciation to Appalachian, it came to refer to the mountains themselves.

Aqueduct Path   *Carter-Moriah Range*

Linking N.H. Rte. 16 with the Nineteen-mile Brook Trail is this path named because it at one time followed an open artificial waterway to the Glen House. This trail is now closed to hiking.

Arethusa Falls   *Pemigewasset-Carrigain*

Perhaps the highest single waterfall in the White Mountains, this cascade on Bemis Brook was discovered in 1840 by Prof. Edward Tuckerman; it was named for him in 1875 by Moses F. Sweetser and J. H. Huntington. But during its history it also came to be known as Arethusa Falls. Some persons suggest this name came from Shelley's poem "Arethusa," which describes a waterfall. But it's just as likely the name was inspired by a nymph in Greek mythology, Arethusa, who was changed into a fountain so she could escape her pursuer, Alpheus, the river god who loved her.

A

Avalanche Brook, from *King.*

Artist Brook, Fall   *Conway-Bartlett-Jackson*

Benjamin Champney (1817—1907) was a nineteenth century landscape painter who deeply loved the White Mountains, and he and several other landscape painters made the mountains, glens, streams, and waterfalls of the region their special province. They were particularly attracted to this brook between Mts. Cranmore and Peaked, and they spent many days painting along it. Champney Brook and Champney Fall on Mt. Chocorua also recall the memory of this pioneer White Mountains artist.

Atkinson and Gilmanton Academy Grant   *North Country*

Two important educational institutions in colonial New Hampshire gave their names to this 13,000-acre expanse of timberland located in northeastern New Hampshire next to the Maine border. These lands were granted to the two academies in 1809 to hold in equal shares and to derive income from them. The academies were named for two prominent Federalist families of the time.

Atkinson, Mt.   940 feet   *Conway-Bartlett-Jackson*

At the south end of Conway Lake is this mountain named for Theodore Atkinson (1697—1779), secretary of the state under the Wentworth governors and a landowner in the town of Jefferson. The town of Atkinson also was named for him. The name Atkinson Mt. appeared on Samuel Holland's map of 1784.

Attitash, Mt.   2,518 feet   *Conway-Bartlett-Jackson*

Now the site of a ski area, this peak is called Little Attitash on the U.S. Geological Survey map; Big Attatish is called West Moat on this map. Attitash Mt. was named by Moses F. Sweetser in his White Mountains guide for the Indian name for blueberries, which once grew profusely on the mountain's slopes.

Avalanche Brook   *Zealand-Twin Mt.*

A

Originally called Cow Brook, this stream on Mt. Webster was renamed Avalanche Brook by two hikers, Henry W. Ripley and a Mr. Porter, because the brook flows near the site of the fatal landslide in Crawford Notch that wiped out the Willey family. Cow Brook, felt Messrs. Ripley and Porter, was too mundane a name for such a tragic site.

Avalon Mt.   3,432 feet   *Zealand-Twin Mt.*

This offshoot of Mt. Field near the Crawford House was thought by Moses F. Sweetser to have resembled the hills of Avalon on the peninsula of Newfoundland. In Britain, Avalon was the legendary residence and burial place of King Arthur.

Aziscoos Lake   *North Country*

The name of this North Country lake straddling the Maine—New Hampshire border is Abenaki for "small pine trees."

Berlin Falls, from *King*.

B

Baker River *Pemigewasset-Carrigain*

Where the Baker River joins the Pemigewasset River was once an Indian resort area. During the years of the Indian wars, while the Indians were engaged in games, they were attacked by a party of whites from Haverhill, Massachusetts, led by Capt. Thomas Baker. Many Indians were killed in the battle, much fur was destroyed, and the name of the victor was given to the river where the battle took place. The Indian name for the river is said to have been *Asquamchumauke*, which in Abenaki means "salmon spawning place."

Baldpate, Mt. 3,812 feet *Mahoosuc Range*

The second highest of the peaks near the Maine—New Hampshire border, this mountain is sometimes known as Bear River Whitecap and also as Saddleback. Baldpate is a common mountain name, derived from the summit being treeless.

Bartlett, Town, Mt. 2,661 feet *Conway-Bartlett-Jackson*

Dr. Josiah Bartlett of Kingston, New Hampshire, a physician whose signature appears just beneath that of John Hancock on the Declaration of Independence, was honored in 1790 by having this town named for him. Dr. Bartlett also became New Hampshire's first "governor," his predecessors having been called "presidents." The town originally had been granted in the 1760's to four officers of the French and Indian Wars, but they never claimed their land so it was later regranted. Bartlett Mt. east of Intervale was also named for Dr. Bartlett (1729—1795).

Bath, Town   *Connecticut Region*

This town between Woodsville and Lisbon was named in 1761 for the prominent English statesman William Pulteney (1684—1764), first Earl of Bath and a brilliant scholar and orator. Poultney, Vermont, once part of New Hampshire, is also named for him.

Bean Brook   *North Country*

Bean Brook is the first stream above Berlin Falls on the Androscoggin River, and it crosses what was once the farm of Benjamin Bean, an early settler in the town of Success.

B

Beans Grant   *Southern Peaks*

In 1831 an act of the New Hampshire legislature authorized the governor to sell previously unassigned public lands, and in 1835 this 3,300-acre mountain area above Crawford Notch was granted to Charles Bean of Maine. Beans Grant, now in the White Mountain National Forest, includes Mt. Jackson (4,052 feet) and Mt. Eisenhower (4,775 feet).

Beans Purchase   *Carter-Moriah Range*

This 33,000-acre tract of wilderness stretching east from Pinkham Notch to the Maine border was purchased in 1832 by Alpheus Bean of Bartlett for $1,000. It was one of the largest grants made by land commissioner James Willey in the 1830's, and it included Mt. Moriah, the Carter Range, and Wildcat Mt. Beans Purchase is now entirely within the White Mountain National Forest.

Beckytown   *Waterville Valley*

In Waterville Valley a woman named Rebekah Blanchard once lived with her husband in the deep woods. From time to time she would get lonesome, so she would walk two miles to the edge of a pasture overlooking a settlement. There, too shy to visit, she would tarry and gaze at the activity below. Local residents became aware of her presence and came to call the clearing where she lived "Beckytown."

Bee Line Trail   *Chocorua Region*

This trail is named because two of its sections make a "bee line" between the summits of Mts. Chocorua and Paugus.

Bemis Lake, Ridge, Mt.   3,706 feet   *Pemigewasset-Carrigain*

The Crawford family, the Willey family, and Dr. Samuel Bemis — around these names revolves most of the history of Crawford Notch. Dr. Bemis was a Boston dentist who spent the summers of 1827—1840 in Harts Location. He was enchanted with the area, and he built a fine stone house in Crawford Notch where he resided fulltime until his death in 1881. The house, known as Notchland, served also as an inn, and it still stands, now called The Inn Unique, which it certainly is.

Dr. Bemis was called "the Lord of the Valley," and he has been described as "one of the most devoted and genial disciples Izaak Walton ever had." He was an enthusiastic explorer of the White Mountains, and the names of Mt. Crawford, Mt. Resolution, and Giant Stairs were suggested by him. In return for his interest, a mountain, a brook, a ridge, and the locality where he lived were all named for him, as was at one time Sawyer Pond near Bartlett.

B

Benton, Town   *Moosilauke Region*

This town on the Wild Ammonoosuc River in southeastern Grafton County was originally named Coventry, but in 1839 Gov. Isaac Hill renamed it to honor his friend, Thomas Hart Benton, U. S. Senator from Missouri, who favored westward expansion. In 1840 the town was incorporated under its new name.

Berlin, Town   *North Country*

Massachusetts, not Germany, gave this industrial city in northeastern New Hampshire its name, and the town's citizens sometimes insist that the name of their town be pronounced with the accent on the first syllable rather than on the second to distinguish it from the German city.

Actually, Berlin began its identity in 1771 as Maynesborough, a name suggested by Gov. John Wentworth in honor of his friend and business associate Sir William Mayne of London, who was associated with him in the extensive trade with the British colony of Barbados in the West Indies. Gov. Wentworth also secured grants in the town for several other Barbados traders.

None of the Barbados grantees of Maynesborough, however, claimed their grants, and following the American Revolution the land gradually was settled by persons from the Worcester County, Massachusetts, towns of Lancaster, Bolton, and Berlin.

Bethlehem, Town   *Cannon-Kinsman*

The name "Bethlehem" for this northern Grafton County town was conceived on Christmas Day in 1799, and the incorporation papers were signed on Dec. 27, 1799, by Gov. John T. Gilman. Prior to this, since 1774, the town had been known as Lloyd's Hills, which commemorated the granting in 1773 of 23,000 acres to James Lloyd of Boston.

B

Bigelow Lawn   *Mt. Washington*

There are several "lawns" in the White Mountains, broad alpine meadows of tough arctic grasses and other flowering plants left stranded by retreating glaciers. Bigelow Lawn on the southern shoulder of Mt. Washington was appropriately named for Dr. Jacob Bigelow (1786—1879), a well-known New England botanist whose *Florula Bostoniensis* was the standard manual of New England botany until Gray's *Manual of Botany* appeared in 1848. In 1816 Dr. Bigelow led an exploratory party up Mt. Washington seeking scientific knowledge. Bigelow Lawn was first noted on Bond's map of the White Mountains, published in 1853.

Black Cap, Mt.   2,370 feet   *Conway-Bartlett-Jackson*

Conspicuous granite patches on its summit are probably responsible for the name of this peak in the Green Hills south of Mt. Kearsarge North.

Blake's Pond   *Connecticut Region*

Moses Blake and Walter Bloss were early settlers of the town of Dalton on the Connecticut River. This pond in the southeast corner of the township was named for Blake.

Blue Mt.   4,350 feet   *Moosilauke Region*

Waternomee was the original name of this peak south of
Moosilauke Brook, but it is later mentioned as Bog-eddy Mt. and as Blue
Mt., the latter name having survived. It appeared as Blue Mt. on Philip
Carrigain's 1816 map of the White Mountains.

Bolles Trail   *Chocorua Region*

Named for Frank Bolles (1856—1894), Secretary of Harvard
University and Chocorua devotee. His chapter "Following a Lost Trail"
in *At the North of Bearcamp Water*, Boston, 1893, describes its re-
exploration on Saturday, July 30, 1892.

Bond, Cliffs, Mt.   4,714 feet   *Pemigewasset-Carrigain*

This peak and associated cliffs were named in 1876 by the
Appalachian Mountain Club for Prof. G. P. Bond, the geographer who
in 1853 made a comprehensive map of the White Mountains.

B

Boott Spur   5,500 feet   *Mt. Washington*

It was over Boott Spur, the prominent ridge running south from Mt.

Bartlett Boulder,
from *Drake*.

Washington, that many of the early ascents of the mountain were made. It is appropriate, therefore, that this ridge is named for Francis Boott, who in 1816 was a member of Dr. Jacob Bigelow's scientific expedition to the White Mountains. Francis Boott was the son of Kirk Boott, founder of Boott Mills at Lawrence, Massachusetts.

The Boott Spur Trail is regarded as the probable route Darby Field took during his ascent of Mt. Washington in 1642. The ridge was called Davis's Spur on Bond's map of 1853, but by 1859 it was being called Boott Spur. The present Boott Spur Trail was laid out by the Appalachian Mountain Club in 1900.

Bowman, Mt.   3,450 feet   *Northern Peaks*

B

The origin of this name is in dispute, with two persons mentioned as possibly having given their names to this northwesterly spur of Mt. Jefferson. The two were Jonas Bowman, an early settler of Littleton and tavernkeeper of Kilkenny, and the Hon. Selwyn Z. Bowman, who while a student acted as an assistant on a mountain survey in the White Mountains.

Boy, Mt.   2,240 feet   *North Country*

Moses F. Sweetser in his White Mountains guide called this scenic viewpoint in Jefferson Boy Mt. W. H. Pickering later wrote that he thought Ball Mt. was the knob's original name. It has appeared on maps under both names. Some people feel the present name is a corruption of Bois Mt., which is derived from the French word for wood.

Bragg, Pond   *North Country*

This pond in the town of Errol was named for the Bragg family, who cleared land and farmed in the early days of settlement.

Bretton Woods   *Zealand-Twin Mt.*

Now the name of a large and famous hotel-resort complex, Bretton Woods was once the name of the town of Carroll, where the resort is located. In 1772 the township of Bretton Woods was granted by Gov. John Wentworth to several persons, including his cousin, Sir Thomas Wentworth, who resided at Bretton Hall in Yorkshire, England. Bretton Hall was the ancestral home of the Wentworths.

The town was settled slowly, and in 1832 an act of the New Hampshire legislature went into effect changing the name of the town to Carroll in honor of Charles Carroll of Carrollton, Maryland, and the name Bretton Woods fell into disuse for about seventy years until the creation of the famous resort.

Bridal Veil Falls   *Cannon-Kinsman*

In his *Heart of the White Mountains* published in 1882, Samuel Adams Drake said this fall on Coppermine Brook, flowing down the north slope of Mt. Kinsman was named because of the "marvelous transparency, which permits the ledges to be seen through the gauze-like sheet falling over them."

Brook Path   *Chocorua Region*

Usually the origin of the name of a place is more interesting than the origin of the place itself. Not so for the Brook Path. This path up Mt. Chocorua clearly was named because it follows Clay Bank Brook, but the path came into being as a way for country people to avoid paying tolls when going to gather blueberries on the upper slopes of Mt. Chocorua. The other routes had tollgates on them under state charter.

Bryce Path   *Conway-Bartlett-Jackson*

This path to the summit of Cathedral Ledge was laid out in 1907 by British Ambassador Viscount James Bryce, whence the name.

Bumpus Basin, Brook   *Northern Peaks*

Silas Bumpus was an early settler of Randolph, and these features between Howker and Gordon Ridges on Mt. Madison are named for him.

Bungy   *Cannon-Kinsman*

Bungy, spelled in various ways, is a place name that occurs both near Colebrook and near Sugar Hill. The origin of the Colebrook name is unknown, but in Sugar Hill "Bungy-jar" is the south wind beginning to blow through Kinsman Notch; when the wind is high, people say "the Bungy Bull is a-bellowing." It is said the wind invariably presages a storm, its high keening increasing in intensity until the storm actually arrives. The term is said to have originated when many early settlers, discovering that they could not farm successfully near Kinsman Notch, departed for better conditions. The remaining settlers said that those who had left had "bunged out."

Burnhams Brook   *Franconia-Garfield*

This tributary of the Ammonoosuc River in the town of Lisbon was named for a hermit who built his cabin near its mouth. As civilization advanced, he left to seek a more secluded locality in the wilderness.

B

Burnt Knoll   *Franconia-Garfield*

The most likely origin for this name is that it comes from the appearance of this knoll near Mt. Garfield following great forest fires here in 1902. Guidebooks nearly twenty years later spoke of the "burned country."

Burt Ravine   *Mt. Washington*

Henry M. Burt was the founder and publisher of *Among the Clouds,* the daily newspaper established in 1877 atop the summit of Mt. Washington. In 1901, the Coos County Commissioners named this ravine paralleling the Mt. Washington Cog Railroad to honor him.

Butterwort Flume   *Zealand-Twin Mt.*

Prof. J. D. Dana and Prof. C. H. Hitchcock discovered this flume in 1875 while they were examining rocks on Mt. Willard for the state geological survey. They named the ravine, most likely for the yellow butterwort flowers they found growing there.

C

Cannon Mt.
from Mt. Lafayette
Bridal Path, from *Drake*.

C

Cabot, Mt.   4,180 feet   *North Country*

Mt. Cabot in the Kilkenny Range is the highest summit in the White Mountains north of the Presidential Range. It was named by the White Mountains explorer and enthusiast William H. Peek for Sebastian Cabot (1476—1557), the sixteenth century English pilot who explored the northeastern coast of North America.

Cabot, Mt.   1,503 feet   *Mahoosuc Range*

On Aug. 19, 1864, a group of guests at the Philbrook Farm Inn in Shelburne named this small mountain north of the Androscoggin River for Edward Cabot of Boston, a longtime guest at the inn.

Cambridge, Town   *North Country*

Cambridge, an unincorporated town located south of Errol, took its name from Cambridge, Massachusetts, where Gov. John Wentworth graduated from Harvard in 1755. The charter was prepared in 1773 but apparently never issued.

Campton, Town   *Pemigewasset-Carrigain*

Two conflicting explanations exist for the origin of the name of this town on the Pemigewasset River. The most widely accepted is that the name is derived from early surveyors and settlers building their camp on the intervale beside the river. As the camp grew, the town took the name "Camptown," and this name appeared on the town's charter in 1761. With time Camptown became elided to Campton.

The other explanation is that Campton was named by Gov. Benning Wentworth to honor Spencer Compton, Earl of Wilmington, who was one of Wentworth's influential friends, so influential, in fact, that it was partly due to Compton's influence that Wentworth became governor in 1741. Wentworth granted this town first in 1761, and it was granted again in 1767 when the name was supposedly given. The difference between Compton and Campton is not necessarily significant, as spelling in the eighteenth century was less formalized than that of today, and the pronunciation of the vowel "a" was broader, as one might expect a Scotsman or an Irishman to speak it today. Thus Compton could easily have become Campton.

Cannon Mt. 4,077 feet   *Cannon-Kinsman*

C Many names have been applied to this peak, which forms the west flank of Franconia Notch. It appeared as Freak Mt., on Philip Carrigain's map of 1816 and as Old Man's Mt. on an 1852 map. It is still widely known as Profile Mt. because on its east side is the famous profile known as The Old Man of the Mountain. The name Cannon Mt. is derived from an oblong rock near the summit that resembles a cannon. Three knobs on the Kinsman Ridge Trail are known as the Cannon Balls.

Cape Horn, Mt. 2,055 feet   *North Country*

An odd squiggle of a mountain southeast of the village of Groveton, this formation is said by some local residents to be named for its resemblance when viewed from above to Cape Horn, South America. Others say it was named for its resemblance to a cow's horn, again when viewed from above. The outline of the mountain corroborates both theories, but one wonders how often the early settlers viewed the mountain from the air. An attempt was made in the last century to have the name changed to Lyon Mt. to honor a prominent railroad official of the time, but the name was rejected by the Appalachian Mountain Club, and time has proved the AMC correct; the railroad official has been forgotten, but the name Cape Horn continues to interest and bewilder people. The name Cape Horn appeared in Carrigain's 1816 map.

Caribou, Mt. 2,828 feet   *Chatham Region*

Located in the town of Mason, Maine, this mountain was called Calabo on the 1853 Walling map of Oxford County, Maine. Its present name doubtless was derived from the presence at one time of caribou in the vicinity.

Carlo, Mt.   3,562 feet   *Mahoosuc Range*

This peak in the Mahoosuc Range was named for a dog at the Philbrook Farm Inn in Shelburne. The dog was a pet and companion of the well-known White Mountains hiker E. B. Cook.

Carr, Mt.   3,470 feet   *Moosilauke Region*

Sometimes a place name preserves in perpetuity the memory of an otherwise insignificant incident, and Mt. Carr is an example. A man once wandered lost for two days in the mountains near the confluence of the Pemigewasset and Baker Rivers before he was finally rescued at Warren. The man's name was Carr. The name Mt. Carr appeared on Philip Carrigain's 1816 map.

Carrigain Brook, Lawn, Notch, Mt.   4,680 feet   *Pemigewasset-Carrigain*

C

Dr. Philip Carrigain was New Hampshire Secretary of State from 1805—1810, but he is more often remembered as a mapmaker. He surveyed much of the state, and in 1816 he published a map of New Hampshire that included many new names, such as Mts. Stinson, Eastman, Willard, and Kinsman. It's probably only fitting, therefore, that several features in the White Mountains bear his name as well. Carrigain was a member of the Weeks-Brackett party of 1820 that named most of the Presidential peaks, and Carrigain Lawn was named for him at that time.

Carroll, Town, County   *Zealand-Twin Mt.*

Wealth and patriotism made Charles Carroll of Maryland one of the best known and respected men of Revolutionary America. He was one of the signers of the Declaration of Independence, and not only was his home town, Carrollton, named for him, but also a town and county in northern New Hampshire that history records he visited only once. In 1776, on assignment from Benjamin Franklin, Carroll made an unsuccessful journey to Montreal to discuss the possibility of a union between U.S. and French-Canadian clergy, and he passed through the White Mountains wilderness en route. The town of Carroll was named for him in 1832, the year of his death; before that the town had been named Bretton Woods. Carroll County was named for him eight years later.

Carter Boulders, Ledge, Notch, Dome   4,483 feet *Carter-Moriah Range*

As happened often in the White Mountains, an explorer interested in botany gave his name to geology. Carter Notch, Carter Dome, Carter Ledge, and Carter Boulders were all named for Dr. Ezra Carter, a Concord, New Hampshire, physician who, in the early 1800's, made frequent explorations in the White Mountains searching for medicinal herbs and roots.

C

The Castellated Ridge, from *Drake*.

Castle Ridge, Castellated Ridge   *Northern Peaks*

Joining Mt. Jefferson from the north, this ridge was named for the rock outcroppings along it known as "castles."

Cathedral Ledge   *Conway-Bartlett-Jackson*

Do you see a resemblance to a cathedral in a large cavity in the face of this cliff? Members of a family named Parsons, who visited North Conway prior to 1859, reportedly saw such a resemblance, and they gave the ledge its present name; before that it had been known as Harts Ledge. Beneath the cathedral cavity is another, known antithetically as Devil's Den.

C

Champney Falls, Trail   *Chocorua Region*

This route up Mt. Chocorua was named for Benjamin Champney (1817—1907), an early landscape artist of the White Mountains who had his studio in North Conway from 1850. The trail was originally built by Prof. J. S. Pray and later cleared by the Chocorua Mountain Club.

Chandler Brook   *Mahoosuc Range*

It seems that any man owning a sawmill on this brook also possessed the right to have the brook named for him. Rising in the mountains east of the village of Milan and running through the town of Success, this brook is said to have once borne the Indian name *Nulliekunjewa*, which is supposed to have meant "great fishing brook." It was later called Stearns Brook for Isaac Stearns who built a sawmill on the brook about 1823, and still later it was called Paine Brook for Henry Paine, a subsequent owner of the mill. About 1850 Hazen Chandler and others bought the town of Success and built several larger mills on the brook, and Chandler's name has survived.

The origin of the name of the Chandler Brook in the Great Gulf is not certain, though it was probably named for Jeremiah Chandler, for whom Chandlers Purchase is named.

Chandlers Purchase   *Mt. Washington*

This narrow strip of land covering part of the western approaches to Mt. Washington, including part of the Mt. Washington Cog Railroad, was granted in 1835 to Jeremiah Chandler of Conway for $300.

Chandler Ridge   *Mt. Washington*

On Aug. 7, 1856, a 75-year-old hiker named Benjamin Chandler left for the summit of Mt. Washington; he didn't return. A year later, on July 9, his body was found beneath a ledge under which he had apparently crawled for shelter and died. The northeast ridge of Mt. Washington where the ledge is located was named for him.

C

Chatham, Town   *Chatham Region*

William Pitt, Earl of Chatham and great English statesman, had sympathy for the American colonists, arguing that England had no right to tax them and should adopt a "more gentle mode" of governing them. Today, the names of three New Hampshire towns honor him — Pittsfield, Pittsburg, and this scenic and sparsely populated town north of Conway, Chatham.

Cherry Pond, Mt.   3,554 feet   *Zealand-Twin Mt.*

This peak appeared on maps as early as 1772 as Pondicherry Mt., but the origin of that name is obscure. Some people say it is derived from the mountain's nearness to Cherry Pond. But others suggest that the name comes from Pondicherry, capital of French India. The city was the scene of frequent struggles between the French and English, and it has been surmised that the name was given to the mountain by French explorers from Canada.

Chickwolnepy Brook   *Mahoosuc Range*

"Frog pond" is what the name of this brook meant in the Abenaki language. Located northeast of Berlin, it's the only stream in the vicinity to take its rise from a pond.

Chocorua Lake   *Chocorua Region*

The same Sokosis chief who gave his name to the mountain also
gave his name to the lake at its base. According to Indian legend, the
stillness of the lake was sacred to the Great Spirit, and the Indians
reportedly believed that if a human voice was heard on its waters the
offender's canoe would sink instantly to the bottom.

C

The Death of Chocorua, after a painting by Thomas Cole, from
Kilbourne.

Chocorua, Mt.   3,475 feet   *Chocorua Region*

As the *History of Carroll County* says, no other peak has been so
celebrated in song, legend, and story. All the legends agree that the
peak was named for the Sokosis chief Chocorua, who lived in the early
1700's. And all agree he met a tragic end on the mountain. The most
prosaic of the stories says Chocorua died on the mountain while
hunting, apparently by falling from a high rock.

But other tales speak of massacre and vengeance. According to
many of the tales, Chocorua's young son died after eating some poison
left out for foxes by white settlers, who had previously enjoyed good
neighborly relations with Chocorua. The chief blamed the settlers for
his son's death, and in revenge slew the wife and children of a settler
named Cornelius Campbell. Campbell and others, seeking vengeance in
their turn, pursued Chocorua to the summit of the mountain, where he
was shot. As he lay dying on the rocks, so the story goes, he said to his

slayers, "Chocorua goes to the Great Spirit — his curse stays with the white man." Soon after, cattle began dying in the region. This, however, was supposedly traced not to the influence of the chief's malediction but to unusually high concentrations of muriate of lime in the water, and a dose of soapsuds solved the problem.

One variant of the story says Chocorua's son didn't figure in the legend at all. According to this version, Chocorua was pursued up the mountain by white settlers seeking vengeance for an Indian massacre, and Chocorua was not shot but leaped from the peak in defiance of his pursuers.

Christine Lake   *North Country*

C   This scenic lake in Stark at the base of the Percy Peaks in Stratford has been called Stratford Pond, Potters Pond, and North Pond. (South Pond, now the site of a state park, is across the valley.) But on Sept. 13, 1883, at their first annual meeting, the members of the Percy Summer Club voted to rename the lake in honor of Mrs. Christine Coates of Phildelphia, the first lady visitor to be entertained at the club's camp on the lake.

Church Fall, Ponds   *Conway-Bartlett-Jackson*

Frederick Edwin Church (1826—1900) was an American landscape artist who visited the White Mountains to paint. This fall on Sabbaday Brook and nearby ponds are named for him.

Cilley Mt.   approx. 2,100 feet   *Moosilauke Region*

The original settlement of Woodstock was on this mountain located about two miles west of the Pemigewasset River. It was named for General Joseph Cilley (1734—1799), a native of Nottingham, New Hampshire, who had a distinguished military career in the Revolutionary War and was later a respected judge and politician. By the Civil War the village named for him was deserted, and now only stone walls show where once cattle grazed. This mountain still bears his name, however.

Clarksville, Town   *North Country*

The lands comprising this town on the upper Connecticut River were originally part of the Dartmouth College Grants, but in 1792 they were purchased by two Dartmouth graduates for a shilling an acre, or $10,000 for eight square miles. By 1820 one of the purchasers, Benjamin Clark, had cleared enough of the rich river valley to attract other settlers, who named it Clarksville in his honor. The name Dartmouth College Grant persisted until 1872, however, when the last of the debt was paid.

Clay, Mt.   5,532 feet   *Mt. Washington*

This northern shoulder of Mt. Washington was named as early as 1848 for the distinguished American lawyer and statesman Henry Clay (1777—1852). While never a President as those for whom the surrounding peaks were named, Henry Clay nonetheless was a presidential candidate several times.

C

Cleveland, Mt.   2,397 feet   *Franconia-Garfield*

Formerly called Round Mt., this mountain southeast of the village of Bethlehem was later renamed for President Grover Cleveland, who summered at Tamworth.

Clinton, Mt.   4,312 feet   *Southern Peaks*

An act of the New Hampshire legislature in 1913 officially renamed this peak, calling it Mt. Pierce in honor of President Franklin Pierce, who was born in Hillsboro, New Hampshire. Mapmakers and hikers, however, paid no attention to the change, and in 1915 the Committee on Nomenclature of the Appalachian Mountain Club recommended continuing the name Mt. Clinton on AMC maps. The original name honored Gov. DeWitt Clinton of New York (1769—1828).

Cold River   *Chatham Region*

Doubtless descriptive, this name is quite old, appearing in the Chatham charter map and also in Jeremy Belknap's *Journal* of 1792.

Colebrook, Town   *North Country*

When Gov. Benning Wentworth granted this town on the upper Connecticut River in 1762, he named it Dryden in honor of the English poet and playwright. Gov. John Wentworth regranted the town in 1770, and he changed the name to Colebrook to honor Sir George Colebrook, a relative by marriage and chairman of the board of the British East India Company.

Coleman State Park   *North Country*

In 1957, the state purchased 1,573 acres in the town of Stewartstown from the estate of Horace C. Coleman to create this state park, and the park was named for him.

C ### Columbia, Town   *North Country*

When this town on the upper Connecticut River was chartered in 1762, it was called Preston. Eight years later it was regranted as Cockburne for Sir James Cockburne, scion of a prominent Scottish family. In 1811, flowing with a tide of national patriotism preceding the War of 1812, New Hampshire Gov. John Langdon renamed the town Columbia. Six other towns in the U. S. have this name.

Connecticut River

White men's names are on the peaks of the White Mountains, and Indian names are on the rivers. This is primarily because the Indians were little interested in the mountains, especially as single units, whereas the rivers were vital arteries. As usual, the antecedants of the name "Connecticut" were spelled and pronounced many different ways at different times, mostly because different Indian dialects were spoken along the river, but they all sounded like "Connecticut," and they all meant "the long river." A 1713 map published in France spelled the name "counitegou." The present spelling appeared on a map as early as 1760.

Connecticut Lakes   *North Country*

These four lakes were named because they are the first major water bodies on the Connecticut River. It would seem the actual headwaters of the river should be called First Lake, but it's the other way around; they're First, Second, Third, and Fourth going north. Third Lake was known by the Canadians as Lake St. Sophia. Second Lake was formerly known as Lake Carmel, for a mountain visible in the northeast.

Conway Lake   *Conway-Bartlett-Jackson*

This pond southeast of the village of Conway was originally known as Walkers Pond. As early as 1766 a Capt. Timothy Walker had a grist mill and a sawmill there, and in 1773 he was granted 100 acres of land bordering the pond and its outlet. The county commissioners of Carroll County later changed the name to Conway Lake, but the old name continued to be used locally for a long time.

C

Conway, Town   *Conway-Bartlett-Jackson*

When the first white settlers arrived in this region, they borrowed the name and possibly the site of an already existing Sokosis Indian village — Pequaket. Darby Field called it Pegwagget when he passed through in 1642 on his way to climb Mt. Washington, and it wasn't long before the name was Anglicized to the unflattering name of Pigwacket.

In 1765 the town was formally named for Henry Seymour Conway (1721—1793), a dashing and ambitious younger son of a prominent English family. But hardly had the new name been given when it was mutated to designate different parts of the town; one section was called Conway Street, another Conway Center, and another Conway Corner. Conway Street, an old farming section near Conway Center, was once known as Fag End.

Conway was also called Dolloftown, after an early settler, and an old psalter found in 1774 has the following rhyme in it:

"Thre men went up from dolluf town,
     And stop ol Nite at Foresters Pockit
To mak ye Road Bi ingun Hil
     To git clere up to nort pigogit.
To Emri's kamp up Kesuk Brok,
     Wha Chadbun is Beginnen."

Cöos County

The largest and northernmost of New Hampshire's ten counties, Cöos County takes its name from *coo-ash*, an Abenaki word signifying pines. A tribe living in the area were known as the *Coo-ash-aukes*, or "dwellers in the place of the pines." Originally, the broad river meadows near Newbury, Vermont, and Haverhill, New Hampshire, were known as "the Cohos," which is how Indian legends referred to them. When the meadows near Lancaster began to be settled, that area was known as "the Upper Cohoss." And still later, when the area around Colebrook was being settled, the famous mapmaker Philip Carrigain bestowed on that region the title of "the Cohoss above the Upper Cohoss."

Cöosauke Fall   *Mt. Washington*

C William H. Peek, early explorer and botanist in the White Mountains, mistakenly thought the Abenaki word *coos* meant "jolt" or "rough," so he joined that with *-auke*, the Abenaki suffix meaning "place," to name this rough place on Bumpus Brook on Mt. Madison.

Coppermine Brook   *Cannon-Kinsman*

This brook running northwest from Kinsman Ridge received its name from the copper mine on its banks. Copper ore was mined there for many years and smelted in the iron foundry in Franconia.

Crawford Notch   *Southern Peaks*

Before Abel Crawford came to the huge defile later to bear his name, Crawford Notch was known as "The White Mountain Notch" or simply "The Notch." Capt. Timothy Nash and Benjamin Sawyer proved around 1772 that a horse could be taken through the notch, but when they had to lower the horse over a cliff with a rope, they also demonstrated how difficult transportation through the notch was (see Nash and Sawyer's Location). Abel Crawford built a path that made the notch accessible to the many explorers who were to follow, and he provided them with accommodations when they came. Abel Crawford lived most of his life in the White Mountains; he explored them, he built roads and trails through them, and he guided and assisted travelers in them. He stood six foot three, and he and his sons dominate the history of the Crawford Notch region. Few persons have had so beautiful and awesome a place named for them, and few have deserved it more than Abel Crawford.

Crawford, Mt.   3,129 feet   *Montalban Ridge*

Dr. Samuel Bemis, who lived in Crawford Notch and was intimately connected with the Crawford family, suggested that this peak be named for Abel Crawford and his son Ethan Allen, early settlers, explorers, and guides.

C

Abel Crawford, from *Drake*.

Crawford Path   *Southern Peaks*

After several parties had visited Mt. Washington, Abel Crawford and his son Ethan Allen saw clearly that a path was needed, so they built one. It was said to be the first path up Mt. Washington, and today it still follows very closely the original route. Begun in 1819, it was first called the Mt. Washington Path, but as other paths to the summit appeared this path came to be known instead for its builders.

Crawford's Purchase   *Southern Peaks*

In 1834 this unincorporated tract of land east of Fabyan's and Bretton Woods was granted to Ethan Allen Crawford and Thomas and

Nathaniel Abbott for $8,000, or less than sixty cents an acre. The land now includes much of the approaches to the Mt. Washington Cog Railroad.

Crescent, Mt.   3,280 feet   *North Country*

The shape of its summit is responsible for the name of this mountain in the town of Randolph. It is referred to on an old U. S. Geological Survey map as Randolph Mt.

Crystal Cascade   *Mt. Washington*

The Ellis River was once known as the Crystal River, and this fall near the outlet of Tuckerman Ravine once shared that name. It appeared as Crystal Falls on Bond's map of 1853 and as Crystal Cascade in Thomas Starr King's book of 1859.

C

Crystal Village   *North Country*

Proximity to Crystal Fall is most likely the reason for the name of this settlement in the town of Stark.

Cushman, Mt.   3,105 feet   *Moosilauke Region*

Nathaniel Cushman was an early settler in the town of Woodstock, and he gave his name to this mountain. The name first appeared on Philip Carrigain's map of 1816.

Currier, Mt.   2,790 feet   *Zealand-Twin Mt.*

Located in the Dartmouth Range west and slightly north of Mitten Mt., this peak was named for Horace C. Currier (1879—1943), a U.S. Forest Service employee who began work in the White Mountain National Forest in 1912 and was noted for his sound forestry practices. The mountain previously had been called Pine Peak.

Crystal Cascade, from *Eastman*.

C

Cutler's River   *Mt. Washington*

In July, 1784, Dr. Jeremy Belknap's party followed this stream
draining Tuckerman Ravine in their ascent of Mt. Washington. The
stream was named for one of the party's members, Dr. Manasseh Cutler
of Ipswich, Massachusetts, (1742—1823). Dr. Cutler, like so many early
explorers of the White Mountains, was an enthusiastic botanist.

Cutt's Grant   *Southern Peaks*

Thomas Cutts of Maine was granted these lands above Crawford
Notch and adjacent to Mt. Washington in 1818. Like similar early
grants, it is now part of the White Mountain National Forest.

D

Dixville Notch, from *Eastman*.

D

CHAPTER FOUR

Dalton, Town, Mt.   approx. 2,000 feet   *Connecticut Region*

D

   This town on the Connecticut River was once part of what is now
Littleton. By 1764 the entire area was known as Chiswick, then in 1770 as
Apthorp, and finally in 1784 as Dalton, in honor of Tristram Dalton,
one of New England's foremost colonial merchants. Dalton Mt., a ridge
running east and west the length of the town, is named for the town.

Dartmouth, Mt.   3,721 feet   *Zealand-Twin Mt.*

   The name for this peak near Cherry Mt. was proposed in 1876 by
New Hampshire State Geologist Charles Hitchcock, who named
numerous other features in the White Mountains. Hitchcock was also
professor of geology and mineralogy at Dartmouth College, a position
he held for forty years.

Davis, Brook, Path, Mt.   3,800 feet   *Montalban Ridge*

   The history of Crawford Notch is largely a family affair. Nathaniel
P. Davis, manager of the Mt. Crawford House, was the son-in-law of
Abel Crawford, patriarch of the region and pioneer trailbuilder. Davis
wanted to build his own bridle path up Mt. Washington, so he started at
Bemis, near the hotel he managed. The path wound up Bemis Ridge, to
Montalban Ridge, and on to Mt. Washington. It opened in 1845 and was
the third bridle path built to the summit.
   The path lost popularity over the years with the arrival of the
carriage road and the cog railway. After fifty years, however, it was
reopened, and today it follows closely Davis's original route.

Deception, Mt. 3,700 feet   *Zealand-Twin Mt.*

In August, 1823, three men from a party staying at the Mt. Crawford House set out to climb Mt. Washington, leaving the women in their group behind. The women, to amuse themselves, set out to climb what appeared an easy and scenic hill to the north. The climb turned out to be much longer and much more difficult than they had anticipated, and one of them suggested the name Mt. Deception for the mountain.

Devil's Den   *Zealand-Twin Mt.*

Among the early settlers and explorers of the White Mountains, the talk was that a cave on the sheer cliffs of Mt. Willard was littered with bones. The cave was called Devil's Den. Franklin Leavitt, the folk mapmaker and versifier from Lancaster, was said to have been lowered into the cave from above on a rope; he saw bones in the cave and refused to enter. In 1870, a U. S. Geological Survey party mustered the courage to enter the dreaded cave — and found nothing.

D

Devil's Hopyard   *North Country*

Some early visitors to this rugged natural ravine near South Pond State Park in Stark were reminded of a hopyard by the vines hanging from trees on the ledges. It's a wild and sunless place, and thus the name Devil's Hopyard evolved.

Devil's Slide   *North Country*

This conspicuous cliff hanging like a stage backdrop to the village of Stark received its name from an Indian legend. The Indians peopled the mountains with invisible spirits, who warred frequently. During one particularly tumultuous battle, one half of a mountain blocking the valley of the Upper Ammonoosuc River subsided into the earth, leaving the valley as it appears today.

Diamond Ponds, River, Ridge approx. 2,800 feet   *North Country*

A moose, not a mineral, gave these North Country features their names. A man named Isaac Diamond, while hunting between the ponds in 1778, shot and wounded a large bull moose. The moose charged him, nearly tearing off his clothes. Diamond dodged behind a tree, the moose kept coming; Diamond fled to another tree; and finally, after reloading his rifle, he shot and killed the moose. From this incident a river, a ridge, and two ponds received their names. The Swift Diamond and the Dead Diamond Rivers were named for their currents.

Diana's Baths   *Conway-Bartlett-Jackson*

These curious circular stone cavities on Lucy Brook were originally known as the Home of the Water Fairies, but sometime before 1859 a Miss Hubbard of Boston, a guest at the old Mt. Washington House in North Conway, rechristened them Diana's Baths, presumably to evoke images of the Roman nature goddess. The pools are also called Lucy's Baths.

D

Dixville, Notch, Town, Mt.   3,482 feet   *North Country*

Col. Timothy Dix and his son, Col. Timothy Dix Jr., in 1805 purchased nearly 30,000 acres in the area of this rugged notch, and in 1811 they were authorized by legislation to construct a roadway through the notch to the Maine border. The project was completed under the supervision of Daniel Webster and his brother Ezekiel, who were then lawyers for Col. Dix in Boscawen.

Dixville Notch — with its jagged cliffs, near-alpine lake, ski area, and stately hotel — today calls itself "Little Switzerland," but to the early settlers it must have seemed like "Little Perdition." Until 1815, John and Betsey Whittemore were the first and only settlers of the region. They had stuck it out three years when Betsey died and John decided to move to Colebrook. The road was not kept open in the winter, and John had to keep his wife's body frozen all winter before he could bury her in the spring. Living conditions in the notch have improved considerably since then.

Dollof Pond   *Conway-Bartlett-Jackson*

Dollof Pond, like Dolloftown, an early name for Conway, took its name from an early settler named Dollof.

Dolly Copp Campground   *Great Gulf*

Dolly Copp began life as Dolly Emery, but in 1831, while still in her teens, she married Hayes D. Copp, and together they built a farm in the wilderness, the site of which is now this campground in the White Mountain National Forest. They lived there for nineteen years and raised four children before they had any close neighbors.

Dolly of necessity was self-reliant, and throughout her married life she made all her own apparel — except shoes. She had tiny feet, and she imported shoes from Portland, Maine. She was famous for her handcrafted linen and woolen articles, and when the Glen House opened in 1852 many visitors came to her farm to see her handiwork and the Imp Profile, visible from the farmstead. She smoked a short clay pipe.

It's said that soon after her fiftieth wedding anniversary she announced, "Hayes is well enough, and fifty years is long enough to live with any man." Whereupon the aged couple peacefully divided their possessions, and she departed to live in Auburn, Maine, with a daughter. Hayes returned to his native Stowe, Maine.

D

Doublehead, Mt.   2,935 and 3,056 feet   *Conway-Bartlett-Jackson*

The name of this mountain northeast of Jackson comes from the peak having two summits. The mountain was called by this name on Belknap's map of 1791. There is another Mt. Doublehead in the Squam Range.

Drake Brook, Ravine, Trail   *Waterville Valley*

Arnold Drake settled in Waterville Valley about 1840, and these features were named for him.

Duck's Head   *Conway-Bartlett-Jackson*

Located on a spur of Iron Mt. west of Jackson, this bluff was named for its shape as seen from nearby pastures. It is also called Iron Bluff.

Dugway Campground   *Conway-Bartlett-Jackson*

This recreation site on the Swift River west of the village of Conway was named because it is near the "dugway" portion of the old Swift River Road, located on the north side of the river. "Dugway" simply means "dug into the bank."

Dummer, Town   *North Country*

A famous fort, a famous academy, and a sparsely populated northern New Hampshire town were all named for the same person — William Dummer, governor of Massachusetts. Fort Dummer on the Connecticut River in Massachusetts is said to have been the earliest and most famous of New England "Indian forts." And Gov. Dummer Academy in Massachusetts was a famous colonial private academy. The Town of Dummer in the North Country was granted in 1773 and was incorporated in 1848.

Durand Ridge   *Northern Peaks*

John Durand was a member of the London Board of Trade and as such had association with the shipping interests of the colonial governor, John Wentworth. Gov. Wentworth was fond of naming towns for political and business associates, and in 1772 he gave to what is now the town of Randolph the name Durand. The town bore that name until 1824, when it received its present name. The White Mountains enthusuast William H. Peek knew the history of Randolph and named this prominent ridge of Mt. Adams for the early name of the town.

Durgin Pond   *Conway-Bartlett-Jackson*

This pond south of the village of Madison was named because James Durgin and his family lived nearby. His wife is buried in a nearby cemetery. The family moved away, but they gave their name to the pond and a clock to the church in Madison.

E

Eagle Cliff and the Echo House, from *Drake*.

Eagle Cliff   *Franconia-Garfield*

A pair of eagles once built their nest high on the sides of this cliff on Mt. Lafayette and thus gave the cliff its name.

Eagle Mt.   1,615 feet   *Conway-Bartlett-Jackson*

This low peak forming the south end of the ridge running from Mt. Wildcat derived its name from its upper crags, once being the abode of "bold and rapacious" eagles.

Eastman Brook   *Pemigewasset-Carrigain*

Amos Eastman was a hunter killed by the Indians near Baker River, and this brook west of Mts. Osceola and Tecumseh possibly was named for him.

Eastman, Mt.   2,936 feet   *Chatham Region*

This peak south of South Baldface Mt. most likely received its name bcause of its nearness to the homestead of the Eastman family.

Echo Lake and Mt. Lafayette, from *King*.

Easton, Town   *Franconia-Garfield*

The name of this sparsely settled town near Franconia appears to be a corruption of "eastern." Until 1867 the town was known as Eastern Landaff, but in that year it was incorporated as Easton.

Echo Lake   *Franconia-Garfield*

There must be hundreds of Echo Lakes throughout the nation, and they all have the same origin for their names: sounds echo freely across them. From the center of this Echo Lake in Franconia Notch at the base of Eagle Cliff, conversations are said to echo two or three times, and according to legends, Indians regarded these reverberating sounds as the war whoops of the gods.

Edmands Col, Path   *Northern-Southern Peaks*

Although dozens of men and organizations have cut trails in the White Mountains, no man is more responsible for the present system of hiking paths than J. Rayner Edmands. Throughout his long life, he labored tirelessly to make the beauty and grandeur of the White Mountains accessible to his fellow hikers.

Edmands first visited the White Mountains in 1868 while still a student at the Massachusetts Institute of Technology. He stayed at Jefferson Highlands, and with several other youths he ascended Cascade Ravine, naming several of the cascades en route. He joined the Appalachian Mountain Club when it was founded in 1876, immediately assuming positions of responsibility within the club; he became the AMC's president in 1886, and from 1894 to his death in 1910 he was one of the AMC's trustees of real estate. He was a professor at Harvard Observatory, and with Prof. E. T. Quimby he triangulated Mt. Washington for the U. S. Coast and Geodetic Survey; during the summers of 1880 and 1881 they worked out of a tower specially constructed on top of Mt. Washington.

E

But it is for his tireless trailbuilding in the White Mountains that Edmands is most often remembered. Edmands mountaineered in the Rockies in 1888 and 1890, and he was impressed by the system of well-graded trails the miners had created there. He returned to the White Mountains determined to create a similar system of trails. He began working in the summer of 1891, going into Cascade Ravine, where he built a shelter, and blazing a trail up Emerald Tongue, the ridge he renamed Israel Ridge. By the next year he had created the system of cairns above timberline whereby hikers could find their way even during heavy fog. The next few years were occupied with constructing trails in the northern peaks, as well as numerous pleasure paths around Randolph and Jefferson. When logging operations threatened to destroy much of his work on the northern peaks, he shifted his base of operations to the southern peaks, but he did not forsake Jefferson and Randolph, for he negotiated with the lumber barons to have their loggers help preserve the trails he had created. Even in his later years, when he was an old man, his trailmaking continued unabated, and in some years he spent on trailmaking more money from his personal account than was contributed from the AMC treasury.

Edmands died in 1910. His goal throughout his long years in the White Mountains was to create trails and facilities that would make hiking possible for persons of all abilities. His trails survive today, and the use they receive is proof of his success.

E The southern peaks of the Presidential Range with Mt. Washington at
left and Mt. Eisenhower at right, from *Oakes.*

Eisenhower, Mt.   4,761 feet   *Southern Peaks*

When the Weeks-Brackett party ascended Mt. Washington in 1820
for the purpose of naming the high peaks for the nation's Presidents,
they encountered a problem — not enough Presidents. They stepped out
of the Presidential league to give Mt. Franklin its name, but when they
came to the next peak they were stumped. Finally, and perhaps under the
influence of the "O-be-joyful" they had imbibed, they gave this
mountain southwest of Mt. Franklin the name Mt. Pleasant. By 1969, the
nation had had Presidents in abundance, and in the year that he died,
Dwight David Eisenhower's name was added to the pantheon of
Presidents honored in the White Mountains. The formal dedication
ceremony was held in 1972 at Eisenhower Wayside Park on Rte. 302.

Elbow Pond   *Pemigewasset-Carrigain*

Tradition says that one Thomas Vincent, a former Revolutionary
War soldier, who in 1875 settled south of Woodstock Center, was
hunting one fall on Mt. Cushman when he spied a pond below.
Returning home, he said the pond had been shaped like an elbow,
whence the name.

Elephant's Head   *Southern Peaks*

This ledge just outside the north "gateway" to Crawford Notch was named because it resembles an elephant's head. Lucy Crawford referred to the ledge by this name in her diary.

Eliot Brook   *North Country*

The name of this brook in the town of Randolph preserves the memory of a settler who made a clearing here before 1800.

Ellis River   *Conway-Bartlett-Jackson*

The origin of this name is unknown, but it has associated with it a charming legend. An Indian family lived near the river's headwaters. They had a daughter possessed of such beauty and virtue that no brave in the area could pass as an acceptable mate for her. One day she suddenly disappeared, and when she was not found, the whole tribe mourned. Later some hunters searching the mountains for game discovered the lost maiden. She was sitting on the shore of the clear mountain stream with a youth whose hair, like hers, floated below his waist. The couple vanished as soon as they became aware of the hunters. But the girl's parents, hearing the tale, knew their daughter's companion to be one of the kindly spirits of the mountain, and they began considering him their son. And he acknowledged the kinship, for they had only to call upon him and he would provide them with whatever game they desired.

E

Elephant Head, from *Bryant.*

The river seems to have been named Ellis, or Ellis's, River for as long as maps have given a name to the river. The earliest mention of the name found thus far is in the grant of land to Philip Bailey, written in 1770.

Ellsworth Pond, Town   *Pemigewasset-Carrigain*

E

This town south of Woodstock has had two names in its history, and both honored men who played important roles in the geographical development of early America. The first name was Trecothick — the only Trecothick anywhere in America — and it came from Barlow Trecothick, Lord Mayor of London and head of the British East India Company. He and others induced the crown authorities to set up New Hampshire as a separate province with its own governors, free from Massachusetts under whose jurisdiction it had been for years. In 1802 the town was incorporated under the name of Ellsworth, for Chief Justice Oliver Ellsworth of Connecticut. That year Justice Ellsworth had negotiated the peace treaty with France that resulted in the Louisiana Purchase.

Emerald Pool   *Chatham Region*

Emerald Pool is a very common descriptive name. This pool near Baldface once caught the fancy of the nineteenth century American landscape artist Albert Bierstadt, and he painted it.

Errol, Town   *North Country*

This town and its name are an odd match. Most of the town is forested wilderness, including the Androscoggin and Diamond Rivers and several large North Country Lakes. From these — logging and outdoor recreation — the tiny village derives its subsistence. It's always been a rugged, frontier sort of place.

But its name comes from a refined aristocratic figure in British history. In 1774 Gov. John Wentworth chartered the town as Errol for James Hay of Scotland, Fifteenth Earl of Erroll, owner of Linlithgow Castle, birthplace of Mary Queen of Scots and King James V. The town was incorporated in 1836.

Ethan Pond   *Zealand-Twin Mt.*

Around 1830 Ethan Allen Crawford discovered this pond southwest of Mt. Willey while he was on one of his many trapping trips, and it was named for him. It is sometimes called Willey Pond, because of its nearness to Mt. Willey.

Erving's Location   *North Country*

This tract of wilderness southwest of Dixville Notch was granted in 1775 to Capt. William Erving of Boston, a soldier in the French and Indian Wars.

Evans Brook, Notch   *Carter-Moriah Range*

Capt. John Evans was one of the original grantees of Fryeburg, Maine, and an experienced Indian fighter. He had been one of Rogers' Rangers, and in August, 1781, following an Indian raid on Bethel, Maine, he was placed in command of an armed guard on the Androscoggin River until winter removed the danger of attack.

The first road through Evans Notch was attempted in 1861 when a narrow road for horse-drawn vehicles was constructed between North Chatham and Gilead, Maine, following what was probably an Indian trail. In hardly a year it had washed out and the route was only a hiking trail until 1914 when the U. S. Forest Service began work on upgrading it, a task they completed in 1936 with help from the Civilian Conservation Corps.

F

The Flume, from *Drake*.

F

Fabyan's   *Zealand-Twin Mt.*

Horace Fabyan's inn was one of the most famous in the White Mountains, and from him is derived the name of this historic site on Rte. 302. Fabyan was a provision dealer from Maine, and in 1837 he built his inn at the northern approach to Crawford Notch. He called it the Mt. Washington House, and he listed among its features his famous six-foot tin horn that he blew each day at sundown. (Just down the road Tom Crawford set off a cannon daily.)

But the site of Fabyan's inn was well-known long before Fabyan arrived there. It was known as Giant's Grave because of a large earth formation that resembled a giant burial mound. In 1791 Abel Crawford bought out the holdings of some settlers, and he set up bachelor quarters in one of their huts. This was occupied the next year by Eleazer Rosebrook, father-in-law of Abel Crawford and grandfather of both Ethan Allen and Lucy Crawford. Rosebrook built a rude teamsters' tavern there in 1803, but it burned. Local legend had it that the site was haunted by an Indian that had declared: "No paleface shall take root here; the Great Spirit whispered in my ear."

It apparently was a potent curse, because when Ethan Allen Crawford put up an inn there in 1817, it burned the next year. In 1819 Ethan Allen Crawford built a two-story tavern on the site, but it too burned. Fabyan's Mt. Washington House lasted thirty years, until 1869, before the curse seemingly claimed it too. In 1872—73 the Giant's Grave was leveled and a large hotel built to accommodate four hundred guests was constructed. It burned in 1951.

The site known as Fabyan's was never incorporated, though it has appeared repeatedly on maps since 1870. Fabyan improved a seven-mile bridle path along the Ammonoosuc River to the foot of Mt. Washington, which became known as the Fabyan Turnpike, then later as Fabyan's Path. Traces of the path can still be seen from points along the Mt. Washington Cog Railroad.

Farlow Ridge   *Chocorua Region*

The list of White Mountain place names includes many examples of geological features named for botanists. William G. Farlow (1844—1919) was a professor of botany at Harvard University, serving as assistant to the famous Asa Gray. Prof. Farlow specialized in mycology, the study of mushrooms and other fungi, and this ridge southwest of Mt. Chocorua was one of his favorite collecting areas. He had a summer home in Chocorua.

Field, Mt.   4,326 feet   *Zealand-Twin Mt.*

This peak near Bethlehem was at one time known as Mt. Lincoln, but it was later renamed to honor Darby Field, who in 1642 became the first white man to climb Mt. Washington.

F

Fishin' Jimmy, from *Slosson.*

Fishin' Jimmy Trail   *Cannon-Kinsman*

The real name of Fishin'Jimmy, for whom this trail to Lonesome Lake was named, was James Whitcher, and he was born in Franconia. But from personal recollections of him by Annie Trumbull Slossum, who wrote a book about him, Fishin'Jimmy is the name he would have preferred. He was a kindly soul, who found both serenity and wisdom fishing in the brooks of the White Mountains. Once when Mrs.

Slossum asked him if he liked fishing, he replied, "You wouldn't ask me if I like my mother — or my wife."

Fishin'Jimmy died, an old man, after he had fallen while hiking to help rescue two boys who had gotten into trouble on Mt. Lafayette. The fall occurred as Jimmy stooped to assist his faithful dog, Dash. His death was widely mourned in the area.

Fletcher Fall   *North Country*

Ebenezer Fletcher, recognizing this fall on the upper Connecticut River in Pittsburg to be a natural site for a mill, built one there in 1811. The Fletcher operations prospered, and the fall was named for him.

Fletcher's Cascade   *Waterville Valley*

On Flat Mt. is a fall named, most likely, for Arthur Fletcher of Concord, New Hampshire, who came to Waterville Valley in the 1870's. The trail to the cascade, probably opened about this time, was destroyed by logging before 1900. It was reopened in 1951.

F

The Flume   *Franconia-Garfield*

It has been called perhaps the most beautiful cascade in the world, and its name simply states what it is — a huge and awesome rock flume. According to tradition, it was discovered in 1803 by 93-year-old Aunt Jess Guernsey; an inveterate fisherwoman, she came across it in her wanderings. (Another version says she discovered the Flume while looking with a tin lantern for a lost cow.)

In 1883, a terrific avalanche dislodged a huge boulder that had been blocking a constriction in the Flume; the passing of the boulder deepened the watercourse and created two new waterfalls.

Flume, Mt.   4,327 feet   *Franconia-Garfield*

Flume Mt., named because Flume Brook flows from it, was originally referred to as one of "the haystacks," as was nearby Mt. Liberty. Early settlers called them this, doubtless, because of their resemblance to haystacks.

The Foolkiller   *Chocorua Region*

Only by looking very carefully on a clear day can a hiker at Passaconaway Campground on the Kancamagus Highway distinguish a ridge whose north slope visually blends closely with that of North Tripyramid. Parties have ascended this ridge thinking they were ascending North Tripyramid, only to find when they reached the top that a long, deep valley and another ridge lay between them and their goal. From this has come the name for the deceptive ridge.

Forist, Mt.   2,046 feet   *North Country*

The cliffs of this peak form a dramatic backdrop on the west for the city of Berlin. The peak was named for a prominent Berlin man, Merrill C. Forist. In addition to holding numerous town and state offices, he also ran the Mt. Forist Hotel, built around 1866.

F

Francis, Lake   *North Country*

The largest water body in northern New Hampshire, this lake was named for Francis P. Murphy, who was elected governor in 1937 and was in office while the dam creating the lake was built.

Franconia, Notch, Range, Town   *Franconia-Garfield*

This region was known as Franconia very early, supposedly for its resemblance to the Franconian Alps in Germany. When Jesse Searle and others were granted lands here in 1764, they called their hopeful settlement Franconia, but the grantees failed to attract enough settlers to build thirty houses, so the grant was revoked. The town was regranted in 1772 — with allowances for "unimprovable lands, mountains, and waters" — and it was renamed Morristown after Corbyn Morris of Boston, one of the original grantees, but the name reverted to Franconia in 1782 after much litigation.

Frankenstein Cliff   *Pemigewasset-Carrigain*

People often assume these cliffs on the west side of Crawford Notch were named either for their towering size or their malice toward climbers and hikers, but the name actually has nothing at all to do with the

Franconia Notch and the Profile House, from *Oakes*.

famous monster. The cliff was named by Dr. Samuel Bemis for Godfrey N. Frankenstein, a young German-born artist who spent much time in the White Mountains and who was fascinated by their rugged beauty.

Franklin, Mt.   5,004 feet   *Southern Peaks*

When the Weeks-Brackett party from Lancaster in 1820 named the high peaks of the White Mountains for U. S. Presidents (see Presidential Range), they soon faced the problem of having more peaks than Presidents, so they named this summit southwest of Mt. Monroe for an American leader of comparable prestige — Benjamin Franklin.

G

Glen Ellis Falls, from *Eastman*.

G

Gale River *Franconia-Garfield*

The origins of this name are obscure. A Mr. Gale once sent a gun to Ethan Allen Crawford from Boston, but no suggestion has been made that this river flowing northwest from South Twin Mt. is named for him. The name appears on Bond's 1853 map of the White Mountains. Galehead Hut, located on a little hump on Garfield Ridge, was built by the Appalachian Mountain Club in 1932.

Gardner, Mt.   2,330 feet *Connecticut Region*

Andrew Gardner, a minister, was an early grantee and settler of the town of Bath. He moderated the first town meeting and came to be known as the town's "patron saint." This mountain separating the towns of Monroe and Lyman is named for him.

Garfield, Pond, Mt.   4,488 feet *Franconia-Garfield*

When President James Garfield was assassinated in 1881, the Franconia selectmen changed the name of a nearby peak known as Haystack to honor the slain President. The tiny pond on the western shoulder of Mt. Garfield had been known as Haystack Lake, but when the name of the peak was changed, the name of the lake lost significance, and in 1918 the Appalachian Mountain Club approved changing the name of the lake to correspond to that of the mountain on which it is located.

Garnet, Hill, Mt.   1,960 feet *Franconia-Garfield*

Garnets embedded in stones are doubtless the reason these two eminences north of the villages of Franconia and Sugar Hill received their names.

Giant's Stairs, from *Drake*.

G

Garnet Pools
Mt. Washington

On the Peabody River near Pinkham Notch are pools in depressions shaped and polished by the abrasive action of water and gravel. The polished appearance of these pools likely accounts for their name.

Giant's Stairs
Montalban Ridge

To Dr. Samuel Bemis of Crawford Notch, these massive terraces between Mt. Resolution and Stairs Mt. suggested giant's stairs, and he proposed the name. The terraces appeared as Giant's Stairs on Bond's 1853 map of the White Mountains.

Glen Boulder Trail
Mt. Washington

This path connecting the Davis Path with Glen Ellis Falls is named for a giant boulder near the lower end of some ledges near timberline. The boulder, which looks as if it's ready to roll down the mountain, is so conspicuous that it can be seen from certain points on N. H. Rte. 16.

Glen Ellis Falls   *Mt. Washington*

These falls on the Ellis River were once known as Pitcher Falls, for their shape. Henry Ripley of North Conway, a longtime enthusiast of the White Mountains, gave them their present name in 1852, and as such they appeared on Bond's map of 1853.

The Indians told a legend about these falls. A daughter of a chief who once ruled this territory loved a youth from a neighboring tribe, but unfortunately her father had promised her to one of his own warriors. To resolve the conflict, the father agreed to a bow-drawing contest between the two rivals. The maiden's lover lost. So, defying their people, the two grabbed hands and fled. They were pursued to these falls, where they leaped to their deaths. It's said that sometimes within the mist the shapes of the two can be seen, hand in hand.

Goback, Mt.   3,523 feet   *North Country* G

According to a journal kept in 1788 by E. W. Judd, this mountain in the town of Stratford was named because of its steepness on one side where all hikers had to "go back."

Goose Eye, Mt.   3,860 feet   *Mahoosuc Range*

No one knows for sure just how this peak in Riley, Maine, got its name. Some persons claim the name is actually Goose High; it's said the geese, in their flights southward from the Rangeley Lakes, fly just high enough to clear the top of this mountain.

Gordon Ridge   *Northern Peaks*

James Gordon of Gorham guided the Rev. Thomas Starr King on the minister's many rambles in the White Mountains, and this northern ridge of Mt. Madison and a nearby waterfall are named for him.

Gorham, Town   *Mahoosuc Range*

This town on the Androscoggin River was originally part of neighboring Shelburne, which was chartered in 1770. The town was named Gorham and incorporated in 1836, actions proposed by Sylvester

Davis, who was from Gorham, Maine, and a relative of the Gorham family that founded the Maine town.

Grafton County

The name of this county forming the western border of the White Mountains region comes from Augustus Henry Fitzroy, an English nobleman who espoused the American cause during the pre-Revolutionary era. Among his titles were Earl of Arlington and Euston, Viscount Thetford, Baron Sudbury, and Duke of Grafton.

Fitzroy was related to Gov. Benning Wentworth, who granted and named the town Grafton in 1761. When his nephew, Gov. John Wentworth, in 1769 designated New Hampshire's five original counties, he named all of them for English parliamentarians who supported the American colonies — and those included Duke Fitzroy.

G

Grange   *North Country*

The Lancaster Grange Hall, once famous locally for dances held there, gave its name to this tiny settlement east of the village of Lancaster.

Gray Knob   *Northern Peaks*

This knob located on the northern slopes of Mt. Adams was named in 1875 by J. Rayner Edmands and William G. Nowell, two noted trailmakers in the White Mountains. The name is doubtless derived from the knob's appearance.

Great Gulf   *Mt. Washington*

In colonial times even more than now a "gulf" meant a great chasm or basin, and that exactly describes this huge basin separating Mt. Washington and the northern peaks of the Presidential Range. The Great Gulf was originally called the Gulf of Mexico, for a reason not known, and it had been observed as early as 1642. In 1829 Ethan Allen Crawford recounted how he once came to the edge of a "great gulf" while wandering lost in the mountain clouds. The basin was formally designated as the Great Gulf Wilderness Area by the U. S. Forest Service in 1964.

Greeley Ledges, Ponds   *Waterville Valley*

These features near Kancamagus Mt. were undoubtedly named for Nathaniel Greeley, who settled in Waterville Valley around 1830 and prospered. He acquired farmlands, built two hotels — one of which burned — and was generally well liked and respected in the region.

Green's Grant   *Mt. Washington*

This unincorporated tract of land adjacent to Mt. Washington just north of the Glen House was one of the last grants made by Gov. John Wentworth to soldiers of the French and Indian War before the Revolutionary War broke out. He made the grant to Lt. Francis Green of Boston.

G

Groveton, Village   *North Country*

A large grove of maple trees once stood where the Groveton railroad station is now located. It's said that when the trees were cut down, the village was named Grove Town, later elided to Groveton. Groveton is in the town of Northumberland.

Gulf of Slides   *Mt. Washington*

Countless landslides have scarred the upper slopes of the broad ravine southeast of Boott Spur, and from these slides the ravine gets its name.

Guyot, Mt.   4,589 feet   *Pemigewasset-Carrigain*

Prof. Arnold Guyot (1807—1884) of Princeton was a physical geographer who wrote learned papers about the Appalachian Mountains, and in 1860 he published a small but good map of the White Mountains. He visited the White Mountains often, and in 1857 he made the first ascent of Mt. Carrigain. In 1876 the Appalachian Mountain Club named this peak north of Mt. Bond in the Twin Mt. Range for him.

H

Hermit Lake and Tuckerman Ravine, from *Bryant*.

H

Hadley's Purchase

Montalban Ridge

In 1834, Henry G. Hadley of Eugene City, Oregon, paid $500 to Commissioner James Willey and received in return one of the hitherto unassigned tracts of land in the White Mountains. Hadley's purchase consisted of slighty more than eight thousand acres, a narrow, mountainous strip of land located above Crawford Notch and east of Hart's Location.

H

Hale Brook, Mt.   4,077 feet

Zealand-Twin Mt.

New Hampshire State Geologist Charles H. Hitchcock in 1874 named this peak in the Twin Mt. Range for the Rev. Edward Everett Hale (1822—1909). The Rev. Mr. Hale came from a well-known Boston family, and in addition to being associated with civic improvement and philanthropic work in Boston, he was also an author whose short story "The Man Without a Country" has become an American classic. According to Hitchcock, Hale "assisted Dr. Jackson (Dr. Charles T. Jackson, a geologist) in exploring the White Mountains, and has done much to make them famous by his writings."

Hale's Location

Conway-Bartlett-Jackson

This 1,215-acre tract of land bordering Echo Lake near Conway was granted in 1771 to Samuel Hale of Portsmouth. No settlement was ever made, and the land is now part of the White Mountain National Forest.

Hall's Stream

North Country

In 1776 an army of American soldiers entered the wilderness of northern New Hampshire in a bold move to invade Quebec. It was a harsh and perilous journey; the soldiers became demoralized, hungry, and exhausted as they traveled, and desertion was rife among the troops. According to one legend, one of the deserters was a man named Hall, who left the army in Quebec and dragged himself as far as a stream known locally as Clear Stream. There he knelt to drink, but he was so weak from hunger and exhaustion that he could not raise his head again and drowned.

Another version of the story says Hall was not a deserter at all but had been left at Clear Stream by his comrades because he was too weak to continue. When the soldiers returned, they found him dead by the stream, and they buried him there. Hall's Stream today forms part of the border between New Hampshire and Quebec.

Hall's Ledge   *Conway-Bartlett-Jackson*

H   The best conjecture is that this outlook located off N. H. Rte. 16 in Jackson is named for Joseph S. Hall, a resident of Lancaster who helped explore Tuckerman Ravine in 1852. As a contractor, Hall was among those persons responsible for the first summit house on Mt. Washington and for the carriage road.

Hammond Trail   *Chocorua Region*

In its *Bicentennial Observance*, the town of Albany noted that this, the oldest trail up Mt. Chocorua, was built by and named for one of the ancestors of Mrs. Ina Morrill, who as of 1966 was Albany Town Tax Collector. The trail begins at the old Hammond Farm.

Hancock Notch, Mt.   4,403 feet   *Pemigewasset-Carrigain*

This mountain was originally called Pemigewasset Peak for its proximity to the Pemigewasset River to the south, but it was later renamed to honor John Hancock, the first signer of the Declaration of Independence. The name of Hancock Notch is also derived from the American patriot.

Hark Hill   1,118 feet   *Mahoosuc Range*

Legend says some settlers living on the Androscoggin River once fled to this hill to avoid detection by raiding Indians. They spent the night on the hill, keeping watchful silence, and the next day they made their escape. As they "harked" for signs of danger, the legend says, the name of the hill was born.

Hart Ledge   *Montalban Ridge*

Col. John Hart, as a reward for service in the French and Indian Wars, was granted lands near the Saco River west of Bartlett, and this cliff in the bend of the river there was named for him.

Hart's Location   *Conway-Bartlett-Jackson*

Hart's Location in Crawford Notch is one of the most historic places in the White Mountains. It was here that occurred the avalanche that wiped out the Willey family, and it was here that lived Dr. Samuel Bemis, who was called "Lord of the Valley." Abel Crawford is buried here. The name Hart's Location is derived from Col. John Hart of Portsmouth, to whom Gov. John Wentworth granted these lands as a reward for service in the French and Indian Wars. The region had originially been called the "Notch of the White Hills."

H

Harvard Brook, Falls   *Pemigewasset-Carrigain*

Located on a branch of the Pemigewasset River, these features were named for their discovery by a group of Harvard College students sometime prior to 1850.

Haverhill, Town   *Connecticut Region*

The majority of the settlers of this town on the Connecticut River were from Haverhill, Massachusetts, and they named their new home for their old one. Haverhill, New Hampshire, includes the broad floodplain through which the Connecticut meanders, and the region was originally called the "Lower Cohoss," from an Abenaki word meaning "crooked." The "Upper Cohoss" was later at Lancaster and still later at Colebrook.

Hawthorne Brook, Falls   *Franconia-Garfield*

Love of nature is a frequent theme in the work of Nathaniel

Hawthorne, the nineteenth century American writer, and this sentiment would have been nurtured by his visits to the White Mountains. His short story "The Great Stone Face" made the profile in Franconia Notch famous. This brook draining the col immediately east of Mt. Garfield was named for him.

H

Cliffs on Mt. Hayes, from *King*.

Hayes, Mt.   2,566 feet   *Mahoosuc Range*

Mrs. Margaret Hayes of Bangor, Maine, was the first proprietor of the White Mountains Station House in Gorham, later called the Alpine House, which was built in 1851 by the Grand Trunk Railroad. This mountain in Gorham was named for her, and it appeared as Hayes Mt. on Franklin Leavitt's 1852 map of the White Mountains. The Rev. Thomas Starr King, whose writings popularized the region, described the mountain as "the chair set by the creator at the proper distance and angle to appreciate and enjoy Mt. Washington."

Haystack Lake   *Franconia-Garfield*

In the summer of 1871 two Dartmouth graduates were assisting Prof. Charles H. Hitchcock in his survey of New Hampshire when they discovered this lake on the northwest side of Mt. Garfield. The mountain at that time was called "The Haystack," and they gave the lake the same name.

Heermance, Camp   *Chocorua Region*

This camp in a sheltered hollow near the summit of Mt. Whiteface was built in 1912 and named in honor of the Rev. Edgar L. Heermance, who has been described as "one of those enthusiastic mountaineering ministers to which the mountains of this whole section owe so much of their history and popularity." Rev. Heermance spent summers in Chocorua.

Hemenway State Forest   *Chocorua Region*

It was from the Tamworth estate of Augustus Hemenway that this state forest was created in 1932, and its name preserves his memory.

Hermit Lake   *Mt. Washington*

In 1853 S. B. Beckett of Portland, Maine, published a guide to the White Mountains, and this tiny lake at the foot of Tuckerman Ravine was named by him.

H

Hibbard, Mt.   3,200 feet   *Chocorua Region*

In the Wonalancet Range southeast of Mt. Passaconaway is this peak named in honor of Judge E. A. Hibbard of Laconia.

Hight, Mt.   4,690 feet   *Carter-Moriah Range*

An early settler named Hight gave his name to this peak adjacent to Carter Dome. Jeremy Belknap's *Journal* of 1792 mentions a Mr. Hight living on Col. Whipple's estate in Jefferson, and it is reported that Hight was a companion of Prof. Ezra Carter on the professor's many explorations in the White Mountains.

Hitchcock Falls, Mt.   2,804 feet   *Northern Peaks, Zealand-Twin Mt.*

Few persons have been more responsible for the exploration and naming of the geologic features of the White Mountains than Prof. Charles H. Hitchcock. The son of a noted geologist, he became a geologist himself, and in 1868 he was appointed State Geologist of New

Hampshire. In that capacity he conducted a detailed geological survey of the state, and his three-volume *Geology of New Hampshire*, which included an atlas, is still an outstanding reference work. He was also professor of geology and mineralogy at Dartmouth College, a post he held for forty years.

Prof. Hitchcock was a tireless and enthusiastic explorer of the White Mountains, and he named many previously unnamed features. In recognition, perhaps, a mountain and two waterfalls were named for him. The fall on Mt. Willard was discovered by Prof. Hitchcock and Prof. J. D. Dana while they were exploring in 1875 for the state geological survey, and the fall was subsequently named for Prof. Hitchcock. A fall on Bumpus Brook north of Mt. Madison is also named for him. And in 1877 Warren Upham honored him by giving his name to a spur of Mt. Field.

H Horne Brook   *Mahoosuc Range*

This brook, which flows into the Androscoggin River above Berlin Falls, is also known as Mollocket Brook (see Molly Ockett). The origin of the name Horne Brook is unknown, but a possible explanation is that it is related to nearby Leavitt Brook (see entry).

Howker Ridge   *Northern Peaks*

James Howker had a farm in Randolph near the foot of this ridge leading to the summit of Mt. Madison. On the ridge are several rocky knobs that have come to be called the "Howks."

Huntington Ravine   *Mt. Washington*

In 1870—71 a party led by Assistant State Geologist J. H. Huntington spent a winter on Mt. Washington, a mountain that has been said with little contradiction to have the worst weather in the world outside of Alaska and the Antarctic. For this feat, Prof. Huntington's associates named this huge cirque on the east side of Mt. Washington for him. In the time of the Rev. Thomas Starr King, about ten years earlier, the ravine had been appropriately called the Grand Gulf, not to be confused with the Great Gulf on the mountain's northern side. In a letter, William Oakes, the botanist, explorer, and writer about the White Mountains, referred to the cirque as "dark ravine," though this reference could have been merely descriptive.

Huntington, Mt.   3,670 feet   *Pemigewasset-Carrigain*

In 1877, Warren Upham named this peak south of Hancock Notch for Assistant State Geologist J. H. Huntington.

Hurricane, Mt.   2,101 feet   *Conway-Bartlett-Jackson*

Presumably a hurricane had something to do with the naming of this peak midway between Intervale and South Chatham, but the exact circumstances have been lost. The peak was previously called Green Mt.

Hutchins, Mt.   3,710 feet   *North Country*

On most maps and guides this prominent peak in the Pilot Range is listed as Pilot Mt. (see entry), but many local residents know the peak as Mt. Hutchins, named for Alpheus Hutchins, an early settler of the region who served under Capt. John W. Weeks of Lancaster in the Battle of Chippewa in the War of 1812.

Campton Village

The gates of Dixville Notch

Nineteenth century photographs, Peter E. Randall collection

Echo lake and Franconia Notch

Franconia and Mt. Lafayette

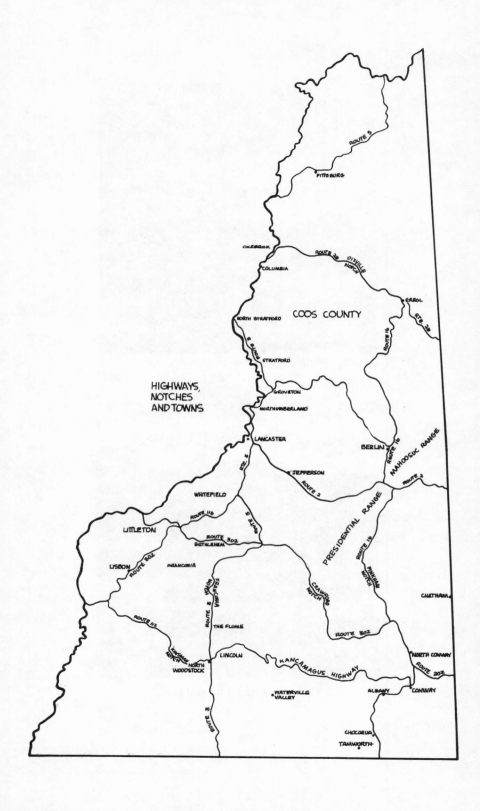

ROUTE 5

PITTSBURG

COLEBROOK

COLUMBIA

ROUTE 26   DIXVILLE NOTCH

ERROL

RTE. 26

COOS COUNTY

NORTH STRATFORD

ROUTE 16

STRATFORD

GROVETON

HIGHWAYS,
NOTCHES
AND TOWNS

NORTHUMBERLAND

LANCASTER

BERLIN

ROUTE 16

MAHOOSUC RANGE

JEFFERSON

ROUTE 2

RTE. 3

ROUTE 3

WHITEFIELD

PRESIDENTIAL RANGE

ROUTE 116

ROUTE 16

LITTLETON

ROUTE 302

BETHLEHEM

PINKHAM NOTCH

CRAWFORD NOTCH

LISBON

ROUTE 302

FRANCONIA

CHATHAM

ROUTE 112

FRANCONIA NOTCH

THE FLUME

ROUTE 302

KINSMAN NOTCH

NORTH WOODSTOCK

LINCOLN

KANCAMAGUS HIGHWAY

NORTH CONWAY

ROUTE 302

WATERVILLE VALLEY

ALBANY

CONWAY

ROUTE 3

CHOCORUA

TAMWORTH

MOUNTAINS,
RIVERS AND
LAKES

CONNECTICUT LAKES

INDIAN STREAM

CONNECTICUT R.

DIAMOND PONDS

MOHAWK RIVER

MAGALLOWAY R.

MUISE MT.

UMBAGOG LAKE

CONNECTICUT RIVER

PERCY PEAKS

ROGERS LEDGE

MT. CABOT

ANDROSCOGGIN R.

MT. STARR KING

MT. WAUMBAK

CHERRY PONDS

MT. MADISON

MIDDLE MORIAH

CONNECTICUT RIVER

MT. ADAMS

PEABODY R.

MT. JEFFERSON

MIDDLE CARTER MT.

CHERRY MT.

MT. WASHINGTON

WILDCAT MT.

AMMONOOSUC RIVER

MT. AGASSIZ

MT. EISENHOWER

MT. MONROE

MT. FRANKLIN

NORTH TWIN MT.

MT. FIELD

MT. PIERCE

OLD MAN OF
THE MOUNTAINS

SOUTH TWIN MT.

MT. JACKSON

MT. GARFIELD

MT. WEBSTER

CANNON MT.

MT. LAFAYETTE

MT. LINCOLN

MT. BOND

MT. RESOLUTION

KINSMAN MT.

KEARSAGE
NORTH MT.

SACO RIVER

PEMIGEWASSET RIVER

MT. MOOSILAUKE

NORTH MOAT MT.

MT. KANCAMAGUS

MT. TECUMSEH

MT. PASSACONAWAY
WATERVILLE
VALLEY

MT. CHOCORUA

MT. PAUGUS

MAD RIVER

MT. WHITEFACE

STINSON L.

Gate of Crawford Notch and the Crawford House

Frankinstein trestle, Crawford Notch

The Willey House

Snow Arch, Tuckerman Ravine

I

The Imp, from *Drake*.

I

Ice Gulch

On the southeast slope of the Crescent Range in Randolph is a long, deep gouge in the earth, and in the trough of the cut are boulder caves that receive very little sunlight and hence remain cool and damp even in summer. Ice can be found in the caves all year long.

Imp Mt.   3,708 feet
Carter-Moriah Range

I

A resemblance to a distorted human profile is what gives this peak in the Carter Range its name. The Imp is best seen from the Dolly Copp Road at the monument marking the site of the Dolly Copp house, and it is said that Dolly Copp herself gave the mountain its name.

Indian Leap
Pemigewasset-Carrigain

Every region, it seems, has a cliff called Indian Leap, named usually for a legend involving an Indian maiden and her lover. But the legend — not involving a love story — behind the cliffs two miles east of North Woodstock is more credible than most. It says that when it was time for an Indian boy to prove his manhood he was taken to this spot on Moosilauke Brook where he had to leap a span of about five and a half feet, with a plunge down a steep cliff the price to be paid for unsteady nerves.

Indian Stream
North Country

This name is unique among White Mountains place names in that it is the only one that also was once the name of an independent nation. That, at least, is how the settlers along this stream near the Canadian border viewed their region when in 1832, disgruntled by the U. S. and Canada squabbling over which nation owned the land, they tried to settle the matter by seceding from both. They formed an

independent nation called the Indian Stream Republic, and they
promptly set about creating their own stamps, coins, government, and
other appurtenances of a sovereign realm. Their little experiment lasted
only a few years, and, by the time of the Treaty of Washington in 1842,
the region had permanently become a part of New Hampshire.

The name Indian Stream comes from Indians remaining in this
region longer than they survived elsewhere in New Hampshire. Before
Indian Stream became the accepted name, the region was known as
Wales Location for a man named Nathaniel Wales, also as Liberty, and
as "Bedel's and Other's Grant."

Ingalls, Mt.   2,253 feet   *Mahoosuc Range*

Located in the Mahoosuc Range, this peak was named for the
Ingalls family (see Moses Rock), pioneer settlers of Shelburne.

Intervale Village   *Conway-Bartlett-Jackson*

An intervale is a level opening in a river valley, and this tiny village
north of North Conway was named for its location on a shelf above the
great intervale on the Saco River. The intervale once was known locally
as Foster's Pocket (see Conway).

Iron Mt.   2,716 feet   *Conway-Bartlett-Jackson*

When iron mines were opened on this mountain west of Jackson,
the name was changed from Baldface to Iron Mt. Iron Bluff on the
summit has also been called Duck's Head (see entry). On June 11, 1915,
the Committee of Nomenclature of the Appalachian Mountain Club
recommended Iron Bluff as the preferred name for the terminus of the
easterly spur of Iron Mt.

Isolation, Mt.   4,005 feet   *Montalban Ridge*

Located near the northern edge of Montalban Ridge, this peak was
named by the White Mountains explorer Prof. William H. Pickering,
doubtless because the mountain is indeed isolated.

I

Israel Ridge   *Northern Peaks*

This northeast ridge of Mt. Jefferson was named around 1891 by J. Rayner Edmands most likely because of the ridge's nearness to the headwaters of the Israel River. Before that the ridge had been called Emerald Tongue, a name suggested by Miss Marian M. Pychowska.

Israel River   *Northern Peaks*

The Indians called this small but vigorous river in Jefferson and Lancaster *Siwoog-a-nock*, meaning "a place where we return in the springtime." Sometime prior to 1750 Israel Glines and his brother John visited the region to hunt, and Israel set up his camp on the river that today bears his name. (John camped near what is now known as the Johns River in Whitefield.) In 1754 another party visited the region, and they named the river for Capt. Peter Powers, a leader of the party who wrote about the river in his journal, but the new name didn't stick. The river is sometimes called Israels River, but this variant has never had official acceptance.

I

J

Mt. Jefferson and the northern peaks, from *Drake*.

J

Jackman Falls

These falls in Kinsman Notch are located at the site of the old Jackman Mill. Jackman was a common name among the early settlers of this region.

Jackson, Town

The first settlers of this town called it New Madbury because most of them were from the New Hampshire seacoast town of Madbury. In 1800 the town was incorporated under the name of Adams, in honor of President John Adams, who was then in office. But the town liked John Adams better than it liked his son, John Quincy Adams, and in 1829, during the presidential race between John Quincy Adams and Andrew Jackson, all the voters in the town except one went with the nationwide majority and voted for Jackson. Soon thereafter, and with the blessings of Gov. Benjamin Pierce, a staunch Democrat and supporter of Jackson, the name was changed to honor the seventh President of the U. S. instead of the second.

Jackson, Mt.   4,052 feet

In 1848 the exploring botanists William Oakes and Frederick Huntington built a fire on the south spur of Mt. Pierce and named the spur Mt. Jackson. Some persons say the peak was named to honor the seventh President, Andrew Jackson, but records of the Appalachian Mountain Club say it was to honor Dr. Charles T. Jackson, New Hampshire State Geologist.

Jefferson, Mt.   5,715 feet   *Northern Peaks*

The third highest peak in the White Mountains was named by the Weeks-Brackett party (see Presidential Range), receiving its name when most of the other peaks of the Presidential Range did. Jefferson's Knees, the peak's truncated eastern ridges, and Jefferson Ravine were named by the early botanist and explorer William H. Pickering. Jefferson Notch on the west was named in 1899 by John Anderson of the Mt. Washington Hotel at Bretton Woods.

Jefferson, Notch, Town   *North Country*

J

This town's first name was Dartmouth, after William Legge, second Earl of Dartmouth, who was the English patron of Dartmouth College and a friend of the American colonies. In 1765, after the close of the Seven Years War, the town was granted to several persons, and among the early settlers was Col. Joseph Whipple of Portsmouth, a wealthy merchant and ship owner who cut the first path through the forests to build his famous "manor." Col. Whipple was an enthusiastic Jeffersonian Democrat, and his brother and partner, William Whipple, was one of New Hampshire's three signers of the Declaration of Independence, a document written by Jefferson. It was through Col. Whipple's efforts and influence that the name Dartmouth was changed to Jefferson — four years *before* Jefferson became President. The village of Jefferson, located on the south slope of Mt. Starr King, is sometimes known locally as Jefferson Hill.

Jennings Peak   3,500 feet   *Waterville Valley*

This peak near Sandwich Mt. is named for "Captivity" Jennings, the baby who was carried off by the Indians to Canada, from where she was ultimately ransomed. The peak also has been known as Dennison's Peak, most likely for an early settler.

Jericho, Mt.   2,483 feet   *North Country*

The origin of the name of this peak west of Berlin is unknown. It was originally called Black Mt.

Jigger Johnson Campground   *Conway-Bartlett-Jackson*

Albert Lewis "Jigger" Johnson was an almost legendary woods boss of the North Country during the region's colorful logging era. For 64 years he was a logger, river driver, and camp boss. Later he became a forest fire lookout on Mt. Chocorua and Carter Dome, spending much time improving trails there. This White Mountain National Forest Campground on the Kancamagus Highway preserves his memory.

Jobildunc Ravine   *Moosilauke Region*

It is commonly supposed that the name of this ravine between Mt. Moosilauke and Blue Mt. is of Indian origin. But in North Woodstock there is a tradition that says the ravine is an amalgam of the first names of three hikers who explored it — Joe, Bill, and Duncan.

Johns River   *Connecticut Region*

This river in Whitefield, like the Israel River in Lancaster and Jefferson, is named for one of the Glines brothers, John and Israel. They visited the area sometime before 1750, and each set up a hunting camp on the rivers named for them. In 1754 an exploring party passing through the region heard the name and, knowing nothing of John Glines, thought the river was named for Ensign John Stark, who had been captured by the Indians while hunting near the mouth of the Johns River. This same John Stark later became the Revolutionary War general who was a hero at the battles of Bennington and Bunker Hill.

Joseph Story Fay Reservation   *Cannon-Kinsman*

This 150-acre tract of forest land near North Woodstock and Lincoln was given to the Appalachian Mountain Club in 1897 by Miss Sarah B. Fay in memory of her father, whose name it bears.

Josh Billings Spring   *Mt. Washington*

Josh Billings (1818—1885) was a noted American humorist and lecturer, and he liked to fish in the brooks near this spring in Pinkham Notch.

K

Kearsarge in winter, from *Drake*.

K

Kancamagus, Mt.   3,728 feet   *Waterville Valley*

This mass of rounded ridges between Mts. Tripyramid, Huntington, and Osceola was named in 1876 by State Geologist Charles H. Hitchcock for the Penacook chief, Kancamagus. He became chief in 1685. He tried to be a friend to the English, but he was abused and mistreated, and he finally led the Penacooks in their last uprising against the white settlers. Then, disheartened and defeated, he and his people retreated to the village of St. Francis, Quebec. Kancamagus was the nephew of the Penacook chief Wonalancet, who was the son of Chief Passaconaway; the place names of the region are all that preserve their memories.

Kearsarge North, Mt.   3,268 feet   *Conway-Bartlett-Jackson*

No small amount of discussion and controversy has focused on this pyramid-shaped peak north of Conway. Not only is the origin of the name complex and obscure, but also the name is duplicated on another New Hampshire mountain located in the town of Warner in Merrimack County, a situation that has nettled generations of geographers and historians.

At least part of the difficulty results from the peak having had a dual identity over the years. It appeared on Thomas Jeffries's map of 1774 as the "Pigwakket Hills," this name clearly coming from the Pequaket Indians who inhabited the Conway region. But Jeremy Belknap's map of 1791 showed the mountains as "Kyarsarge," and it has been suggested that Belknap took the name from a still earlier map. John Farmer and Jacob B. Monroe, in their *Gazeteer of the State of New Hampshire* published in 1823, referred to the mountains as "Piquawket." The Rev. Thomas Starr King, writing in the 1850's, believed the original name of the mountain was Pequaket, though he personally advocated changing the name of the "queenly mountain" to Martha Washington.

Yet during and despite all this, the local inhabitants of the Conway region were calling the mountain "Kiarsarge," and when the old Pequaket Indian Sabatis was asked the Indian name of the peak, he replied *Ke-sough* or *Ke-a-sock*, Indian pronunciations not being easily fitted to English spellings.

The smoldering confusion and contention about the name were fanned by the existence of the other Mt. Kearsarge in Warner, and in 1876 it was proposed to change the name of the northern peak. The move failed, but not before Conway residents became very exercised over the issue. At the time the Conway judge, Joel Eastman, wrote: "All, from the oldest to the youngest, still call the mountain Kiarsarge, throughout this section of the country, and any attempt to change the name will be futile. It will still go by the name of Kiarsarge until the Day of Judgment, and afterwards, if the memory of things of this world remain after that day . . ."

It's too early yet to tell about Judgment Day, but so far Judge Eastman was correct about the durability of the name Kearsarge. Although the U. S. Geographical Board officially adopted the name Pequawket for the mountain in 1915, it continued to be called Kearsarge, and finally, in 1958, a compromise solution was reached, with it being agreed in both Concord, New Hampshire, and Washington, D.C., that the peak in Warner be called Mt. Kearsarge and the northern peak be called Mt. Kearsarge North.

K

But from where came the name Kearsarge? The most imaginative theory was that it came from a hunter named Hezekiah Sargent who frequented the southern peak in the mid-1700's. The name was thought to have been derived from a popular contraction of his name, the mountain being called "Kiah Sarge's Mountain." Subsequent research, however, has questioned the hunter's existence and more decisively has found that the name Kearsarge was in use before 1725, a full quarter century before the hunter was in the area.

An Indian origin of the name is the likeliest possibility. It's not known what the old Pequaket, Sabatis, said the name meant to him, and without his authority we're left with numerous other translations. One is that the name comes from *kesarzet*, an Abenaki word meaning "the proud or selfish," and the peak does indeed stand aloof and alone. Kearsarge can also be translated into Abenaki to mean "pointed mountain," "high place," and "land that is harsh, rough, and difficult" — all also valid descriptions. Another Abenaki word the name is thought to be derived from is *Cowsischewaschook*, a title the Abenakis are supposed to have applied to the mountain, and meaning "notch-pointed mountain of pines." Other persons have said the name is simply a euphonization of two Abenaki descriptive words, *kees* meaning "high," and *-auke*, a suffix meaning "place." And the History of Carroll County says the name doesn't come from Abenaki at all but from *ke-*

sough, an Algonquin word meaning "born of the hill that first shakes hands with the morning light."

Any — or none — of these explanations may be correct.

Kidderville   *North Country*

Around 1830 a man named Moody Little built a sawmill near the site of this hamlet east of Colebrook. Soon after, the sawmill was purchased and refitted by Abial Kidder, and the little settlement has borne his name ever since.

Kilkenny, Town   *North Country*

County Kilkenny in eastern Ireland shares its name with this unincorporated, uninhabited town containing Mt. Cabot, the highest peak north of the Presidential Range. The town was not always uninhabited, but in the 1820's the writer John Farmer described Kilkenny as having "very few inhabitants and they are very poor and for aught that appears to the contrary they must remain so as they may be deemed actually trespassers on that part of God's heritage which he designed for the reservation of bears, wolves, moose, and other animals of the forest." Nothing much has happened since then to alter Farmer's assessment.

K

Kimball Brook   *North Country*

George Kimball came to the town of Stratford around 1812, and this small brook flowed through his farm.

Kimball Ponds   *Chatham Region*

The origin of the name of these ponds northeast of South Chatham is unknown, but they first appeared on Samuel Holland's 1784 map as "Kimball's Ponds."

Kineo, Mt.   3,320 feet   *Moosilauke Region*

In Abenaki *kineo* means "sharp peak," whence the name of this peak located east of Warren.

King Ravine, from *King*.

K

King Ravine   *Northern Peaks*

The Rev. Thomas Starr King, the White Mountains explorer and publicist, in 1857 led the first party to explore this huge cirque on the north side of Mt. Adams. In his book, *The White Hills*, Boston, 1859, the Rev. Mr. King called the huge bowl Adams Ravine, but it later came to bear his own name instead.

Kinsman Notch, Mt.   4,363 feet   *Cannon-Kinsman*

Asa Kinsman and his wife arrived in the town of Easton in the 1780's with all their belongings piled on a two-wheeled cart pulled by a yoke of oxen, and they literally had to hew their way through the wilderness to take up their claim. Kinsman is buried in a little cemetery in Easton.

L

Mt. Lafayette, from *Drake*.

L

Ladd Pond   *North Country*

Daniel Ladd settled near this pond in Stewartstown and gave his name to it. The pond was well-known for the "loup-cervier," or Canadian lynx, that frequented it, and Ladd and his son David set about exterminating them, partly to be rid of them and partly for the bounty.

Lafayette, Mt.   5,249 feet   *Franconia-Garfield*   L

This peak east of Franconia Notch was originally called the Great Haystack by early settlers because of its shape, and the smaller peaks nearby — Liberty and Flume — were simply called the Haystacks. Rev. Timothy Dwight (1752—1817), president of Yale University who led two trips to the mountain, once proposed naming the mountain Wentworth after New Hampshire's last colonial governor, John Wentworth, but nothing came of his idea.

The mountain received its present name as a way of honoring the visit to America in 1824—25 of the French nobleman, the Marquis de LaFayette, who came to the aid of the colonists during the Revolutionary War. In 1826 the following letter signed by "R.S." appeared in the Boston *Courier* newspaper: "On the last anniversary of the Battle of Yorktown, a respectable assemblage of the citizens of Franconia and the neighboring towns, with due formality, dedicated this mountain to the name of the illustrious hero of that day, LaFayette."

Lakes of the Clouds   *Mt. Washington*

These two tiny alpine ponds in the col between Mt. Monroe and Mt. Washington were called Blue Ponds by the Weeks-Brackett party in 1820 (see Presidential Range), a name facetiously thought to be derived from the "O-be-joyful" the party's members were known to have consumed

L

Lakes of the Clouds, from *Drake*.

that day. The lakes were later called Washington's Punch Bowl. The present name had been given to the ponds as early as 1831, and they are indeed lakes of the clouds, the larger pond being at an elevation of 5,050 feet.

Lancaster, Town   *North Country*

Lancaster is the county seat of Coos County. Its name was suggested by Joseph Wilder, an early settler who, along with many other settlers of the area, had come from Lancaster, Massachusetts. A party of men, mostly from Lancaster, ascended the Presidential Range in 1820 and gave most of the peaks the names they bear today.

Landaff, Town   *Cannon-Kinsman*

Landaff, located east of Lisbon, was originally granted as Whicherville in 1764, but in 1774 it was reincorporated as Llandaff. This early spelling is clearly Welsh, and the second "l" has been dropped over the years. The town received its name in honor of the Bishop of Llandaff, who at that time was chaplain to King George III of England. The town was proposed as the site for Dartmouth College, but local landowners proved too stubborn in relinquishing their land claims. The name Llandaff Mt. appeared on Philip Carrigain's map of 1816.

Lancaster and the Presidential Range, from *King*.

Langdon, Mt.   2,423 feet   *Montalban Ridge*

Langdon Mt. in the southern portion of Montalban Ridge was at one time named Mt. Blackwell by Lucy Stone Blackwell to honor her husband, Henry B. Blackwell. In 1876 the Appalachian Mountain Club renamed the peak to honor Dr. Samuel Langdon, president of Harvard College, and joint author with Col. Blanchard of a map of New Hampshire.

Leadmine Brook, Reservation   *Mahoosuc Range*

Lead was discovered about 1820 near this brook roughly halfway between Gorham and Shelburne, and the lead mine that was opened soon after the discovery gave the brook its name. A piece of ore from the mine, weighing about 2,400 pounds and nearly cubical in shape, was exhibited in London in 1851 and was said to be the largest piece of pure galena ever mined. In 1835 Miss Anne Whitney of Boston and Mrs. Grace E. Kendall of New York gave 155 acres on both sides of the Androscoggin River to New Hampshire to be used as a public reservation, and the tract also took the name of the mine.

Leavitt Brook   *North Country*

In the winter of 1818 two boys, William Horne (see Horne Brook) and Edmund Leavitt, ran away from their homes in Stark, intending to follow the Androscoggin River South to Shelburne. Deep snow hindered their progress, and it was after dark before they could hear Berlin Falls. Fearing that they could not get safely around the falls, they abandoned their plans and turned homeward. At the mouth of a small brook, Leavitt collapsed from cold and exhaustion. Horne, unable to move Leavitt, left him there to go for help. He finally reached the farm of Moses Robbins, the only settler nearby, but when a rescue party reached Leavitt they were too late; he had died. The brook where he perished took his name. There is a Horne Brook nearby that may have been named for his companion.

Jim Liberty Shelter   *Chocorua Region*

James Liberty was an enterprising Frenchman who lived most of his life in the White Mountains. In 1887 he and some other local residents improved an old trail up Mt. Chocorua and set about charging a toll of twenty-five cents to use it. They built a stone camp beneath the peak, but high winds blew off the canvas roof, and timber for another roof had burned, so they set up a bunch of tents inside the stone walls. When the tents were full, "lodgekeeper" Liberty slept under the sky on a bed of hemlock boughs. He would signal his presence at the camp by lighting a fire that could be seen from the valley below, and he would welcome guests by brewing them some strong green tea and singing strange French songs to them while he played the accordion and puffed on an old clay pipe. In 1892 David Knowles built a two-story hotel known as the Peak House, which stood until it was felled by high winds in 1915. The stone stable was rebuilt by the Chocorua Mountain Club in 1924 and named the Jim Liberty Shelter. In 1932 strong winds again damaged the structure, but it was replaced in 1934 by the U. S. Forest Service.

Liberty, Mt.   4,460 feet   *Franconia-Garfield*

L

Mt. Liberty, Mt. Lafayette, and Mt. Flume were all known to early settlers as "the haystacks," because of their shapes. Lucy Crawford, wife of Ethan Allen Crawford, referred in her diary to being able to see to the south of her home at Fabyan's "the beautiful green hill were deer live in the summer, since named Liberty Mountain. . . ." But it is not known which mountain she was speaking about because the summit that today bears that name could not be seen from Fabyan's, and deer certainly could not be seen on its slopes. An article in *Harper's Magazine* mentioned the Mt. Liberty in the Franconia Range in 1852. It is not known how or why Mt. Liberty received its name.

Lincoln Mt.   5,108 feet   *Franconia-Garfield*

A Mr. Fifield named this peak in the Franconia Range for President Abraham Lincoln. It had previously been called Mt. Pleasant.

Lincoln, Town   *Pemigewasset-Carrigain*

The town of Lincoln was named in 1764 for Henry Clinton, Ninth Earl of Lincoln and a cousin of the Wentworths. Lincoln was once the site of intense lumbering activity, and loggers dubbed parts of the region with names such as Pullman, Sawdust Boulevard, and Henryville, the last name derived from the Henry Co., established in 1892 by J. E. Henry to carry out logging operations in the area; the whole region was once facetiously referred to as the "Grand Duchy of Lincoln."

The Link   *Northern Peaks*

J. Rayner Edwards in 1893 built this path skirting the lower northern slopes of Mts. Madison, Adams, and Jefferson. He intended it to be a connecting "link" between the Ravine House and the paths ascending Nowell, Israel, and Castellated Ridges.

Lion Head   *Mt. Washington*

Originally known as St. Anthony's Nose, this rocky prominence on the southeast shoulder of Mt. Washington has been known since about 1875 as Lion Head, a name derived from its shape.

L

Lisbon, Town   *Cannon-Kinsman*

Lisbon is the fourth name this town south of Littleton has borne during its history. It was originally named Concord in 1763, then renamed Chiswick a year later. Three years after that it was renamed again, as Gunthwaite. It was named Lisbon in 1824, most likely at the suggestion of Gov. Levi Woodbury. His friend, Col. William Jarvis, had been consul at Lisbon, Portugal, during Jefferson's administration and was largely responsible for 3,500 merino sheep being sent to the U. S., many to New Hampshire.

Little Haystack Mt.   4,513 feet   *Franconia-Garfield*

Early settlers referred to Mt. Liberty, Mt. Flume, Mt. Lafayette, and this peak as "the Haystacks," a name derived from their shapes. Mt. Lafayette was known as the "Great Haystack."

Littleton, Town   *Franconia-Garfield*

Until 1770 this town was a part of Lisbon, which was then called Chiswick. In that year the town was granted by Gov. John Wentworth as Apthorp to a group of wealthy Boston merchants who purchased or were granted 40,865 acres in the White Mountains. About the time of the

Revolutionary War, these lands came into the possession of Col. Moses Little, "Surveyor of the King's Woods" under Gov. Wentworth and a veteran of the French and Indian Wars and the Battle of Bunker Hill. Littleton was named for him in 1784, the same year New Hampshire became a state.

Livermore, Town   *Conway-Bartlett-Jackson*

Almost all traces have vanished of the once-thriving lumber settlement that existed in this unincorporated town six miles west of Bartlett. The town had been incorporated in 1876, and it was named for Samuel Livermore, an early grantee of the town and first Chief Justice of New Hampshire. But its population dwindled during this century, reaching zero by 1951 when its incorporation was revoked.

Lonesome Lake   *Cannon-Kinsman*   L

Formerly known as Tamarack Pond and as Moran Lake, the lake beneath the south shoulder of Cannon Mt. was given its present name by the author and editor William C. Prime (1825—1905), who had a cabin on its shores.

Long, Mt.   3,615 feet   *North Country*

The shape of this mountain in Stratford, especially when viewed from the west, is doubtless responsible for its name. The name Long Mt. appears on a 1788 map of Stratford.

Lost Nation   *North Country*

Next to the Pilot Range east of Lancaster is this tiny settlement that was neither lost nor a nation. Local tradition says the locality received its name from an incident in which a traveling preacher visited the area and called the people together for worship. Only one person showed up, so the preacher likened the local residents to one of the lost tribes of Israel. A less common tradition says the name was derived from an early pack peddler finding travel in the area so difficult because of the rough roads that he dubbed the area "Lost Nation."

Lost River   *Moosilauke Region*

It's not surprising that this river on Mt. Moosilauke is called Lost River because as it tumbles down the mountain through a boulder-filled gorge it has little choice but to "disappear" from time to time among the huge rocks and potholes. A very credible local tradition says that the river was "found" by two young boys, Royal and Lyman Jackman, who went fishing in the valley one day. Suddenly, Royal later related, Lyman disappeared "as though the earth had opened and swallowed him." He'd dropped a dozen feet through a hole into a waist-deep pool. Badly frightened but unhurt he was fished out by Royal. Many years later the aged Royal returned to North Woodstock. While there he blazed a trail through the woods with the help of some local boys, and when it was finished he took the boys to what is now the Cave of the Shadows. "This," he said, "is where my brother found the Lost River."

Actually, many persons have claimed to have "found" Lost River, and exactly who first explored the stream can never be determined.

L

Lowe and Burbank Grant   *Northern Peaks*

In 1832 Clovis Lowe of Jefferson and Barker Burbank of Shelburne purchased from the state this tract of land that includes Mt. Madison, Mt. Sam Adams, and Pine Mt. The land is now within the White Mountain National Forest.

Lowe's Path   *Northern Peaks*

Leading from Bowman Station in Randolph over Nowell Ridge to the summit of Mt. Adams, this path was made by Charles E. Lowe in 1875—76 from his house on Randolph Highway, and until 1880 he maintained it as a toll path. Lowe was a well-known guide in the region, and from 1895 to his death in 1907 he was the proprietor of the Mt. Crescent House at Randolph. Lowe was assisted in building the path named for him by William G. Nowell, a very active trailmaker in the White Mountains.

Lowell Mt. 3,743 feet   *Pemigewasset-Carrigain*

Originally called Brickhouse Mt., this peak northeast of Carrigain Notch was renamed in 1869 by the N. H. Geological Survey for Abner Lowell of Portland, Maine, an old and enthusiastic explorer of the White Mountains.

Lyman, Town

In 1761 this town in northwestern Grafton County was granted to Daniel Lyman and sixty-three others, ten of whom were also named Lyman.

L

M

Marshfield, from *Drake*.

M

Mad River   *Waterville Valley*

On the back of the original charter of Thornton, dated 1768, is a rough map on which the "Madd River" appears. The difference in spelling between "Madd" and "Mad" is inconsequential, as orthography during that time was a matter of individual preference, and unfortunately the antiquity of the name offers no clues to its origin. **M**

The poet Henry Wadsworth Longfellow wrote a poem entitled "Mad River in the White Mountains." One of the stanzas goes like this:

> "Men call me Mad, and well they may,
> When, full of rage and trouble,
> I burst my banks of sand and clay,
> And sweep their wooden bridge away,
> Like withered reeds or stubble."

Madison, Mt.   5,363 feet   *Northern Peaks*

The most northerly peak of the Pesidential Range was named in 1820 by the Weeks-Brackett party from Lancaster (see Presidential Range) in honor of the nation's fourth President, James Madison (1751—1836). Madison Spring located nearby was named by William G. Nowell in 1875.

Magalloway River, Mt.   3,360 feet   *North Country*

Magalloway in the Abenaki language means "the shoveler" and refers to the caribou. The Abenakis called the caribou "shovelers" because of their habit of shoveling snow aside with their hooves to get food. So a loose translation of the name of this river in northeastern Cöos County would be "dwelling place of the caribou."

Mahoosuc Notch, Range   *Mahoosuc Range*

Clearly of Indian origin, there are two possible translations of this name, both equally probable. In Abenaki, the word means "abode of hungry animals," a phrase that could refer to bears or wolves. And it has been suggested that the name in the region refers to the Mohegan-Pequot refugees who fled from Connecticut to Maine following the Pequot War of 1637.

But the word also translates into the Natick Indian language to mean "pinnacle" or "mountain peak," which aptly describes the region. The Appalachian Mountain Club in 1918 approved the name for the range of mountains running from the Androscoggin River valley at Gorham to Grafton Notch in Maine. The name had previously been applied just to Mahoosuc Notch.

M **Marshfield Station**   *Southern Peaks*

The first white man to ascend Mt. Washington was Darby Field, and the first, and only, man to put a railroad up it was Sylvester Marsh. From the joining of their two surnames came the present name for the train station servicing the Mt. Washington Cog Railroad. The station had previously been known as Kroflite Kamp.

Martin Meadow Pond   *North Country*

An early hunter named Martin is the origin of the name of this pond located south of the village of Lancaster. The names Martin Meadow and Martin Meadow Hills appeared on Philip Carrigain's 1816 map of the White Mountains.

Martin's Location   *Great Gulf*

Thomas Martin of Portsmouth, New Hampshire, was a conductor of artillery stores in the French and Indian Wars, and in 1773 he was among the original grantees of this tract of land in Pinkham Notch. The lands were never incorporated, and today they are notable for being the site of the Dolly Copp Campground.

McGrillis Path   *Chocorua Region*

The site of the McGrillis Farm is located near this path up Mt. Whiteface.

Meserve Brook   *Conway-Bartlett-Jackson*

Prior to 1915 considerable confusion had existed as to the name of this brook running into the Ellis River west of Jackson and the name of the brook roughly paralleling it on the north. In that year, the Committee on Nomenclature of the Appalachian Mountain Club recommended that the brook running from Maple Mt. be called Meserve Brook and the other one Miles Brook. The name Meserve most likely comes from W. A. Meserve of Jackson, who in 1905 built the path to nearby Iron Mt.

Metallak Island, Mt.   2,699 feet   *North Country* **M**

Metallak was a chief of the Coo-ash-auke Indians who once inhabited the northern tip of New Hampshire. Legend tells that when his wife (see Moll's Rock) died, he put her body into a canoe and went with it down rapids on the Androscoggin River until he came to the island that bears his name. There, where he buried her, he built a hut where he lived in solitude. Several years later, in 1846, he was found, blind and starving, by some hunters. They took him to Stewartstown where he lingered for a few years, a ward of the state. He was buried in a tiny cemetery in Stewartstown, the last of his people. This peak in Millsfield preserves his memory.

Milan, Town   *North Country*

When this town on the upper Androscoggin River was originally granted in 1771, it was called Paulsbourg, for Gov. John Wentworth's cousin Paul, who resided in England. Few settlers were attracted to the region, but they included relatives of Milan Harris, whose family members were among the persons who established the first woolen mills in the U. S., at Harrisville, New Hampshire. Gov. Levi Woodbury was a friend of Milan Harris, and the governor was interested in encouraging the wool business in the state, so in 1824 he authorized changing the name of this town to Milan for the first name of his friend, his surname already having been given to another town.

Miles Brook   *Conway-Bartlett-Jackson*

The name of this brook running southeasterly from Rocky Branch Ridge into the Ellis River has often been mistakenly given to the brook paralleling it to the south, Meserve Brook. In 1915 the Appalachian Mountain Club's Committee on Nomenclature recommended the present designation. Winniweta Falls are on Miles Brook.

Millen Hill   approx. 3,300 feet   *Northern Peaks*

People living in Jefferson Highlands often refer to this peak immediately east of Jefferson Peak as Little Bowman, probably because of its proximity to Bowman Mt. But in 1915, the Appalachian Mountain Club's Committee on Nomenclature recommended that it bear the name Millen Hill. The mapmaker Samuel Holland, in preparing his map of the White Mountains in 1773—74, mistakenly applied the name Millen Mt. to nearby Mitten Mt., seemingly because of an error by an engraver. The origin of the name Millen Hill is unknown.

M

Millsfield, Town   *North Country*

Located southeast of Dixville Notch, this sparsely populated town was named for Sir Thomas Mills of London, a prominent trader in lumber and other commodities and an advocate in Parliament of conciliation with the New England colonies. The town was granted by Gov. John Wentworth in 1774, but it was never incorporated, and by 1960 the population, never large, had dwindled to seven.

Mist Mt.   approx. 2,100 feet   *Moosilauke Region*

Mist sweeping upward from nearby Lake Tarleton in Piermont to the summit of this peak supposedly is responsible for the mountain's name.

Mitten Mt.   3,050 feet   *Zealand-Twin Mt.*

More than once in White Mountains history a seemingly trivial incident gave rise to an enduring and intriguing name, and the name of this mountain in the Dartmouth Range provides an example. In April, 1771, according to tradition, 30-year-old Timothy Nash was following a moose through the dense forest on this mountain when he lost his bearings. He climbed a tree to get a better view when he saw to the south the huge cleft in the mountains that was later to be called Crawford Notch. In climbing the tree, Nash lost a mitten, and for over two centuries the name Mitten Mt. has recalled that incident.

But while the losing of the mitten may have been trivial, the discovery of Crawford Notch was important indeed (see Nash and Sawyer's Location). The settlers of Lancaster and nearby towns would have preferred to have taken their trade goods to Portsmouth or Portland, but the White Mountains barred their way; instead they had to travel fifty miles down the Connecticut River to Haverhill, an easy journey down but a difficult one back, and farther from the markets they wanted. For years the settlers had dreamed of one day finding a route that could take them through the White Mountains to Conway, and in 1767 the hoped-for discovery of such a route was discussed at a meeting of Lancaster's proprietors; Timothy Nash was at that meeting, So, when Nash spied Crawford Notch on that April day over 200 years ago, he had reason to forget about his mitten.

The name Mitten Mt. first appeared on the 1772 charter map of Bretton Woods.

M

Moat Mt., from *Drake*.

Moat Mt.   3,201   *Conway-Bartlett-Jackson*

Moat Mt., an irregular ridge west of the Saco River nearly opposite North Conway, is actually three mountains: North Moat (3,201 feet), Middle Moat (2,760 feet), and South Moat (2,772 feet). It was called Moat Mt. by early settlers because of beaver dams along streams on the mountain's slopes. The ponds behind the dams were called "moats" locally, and a visit to the region was termed "going over the moats." The name appears spelled "Mote" on the 1771 charter map of Albany.

Mohawk River   *North Country*

Mohawk Indians are supposed to have raided in this region in early times, and settlers named this river paralleling N. H. Rte. 26 east of Colebrook for them.

M

Moll's Rock   *North Country*

"Molly Molasses" was supposedly a nickname the Coo-ash-auke chief Metallak (see Metallak Island) used for his wife. This islet in the town of Errol is named for her.

Molly Ocket

Molly Ocket was an old Pequaket Indian woman who lived and traveled throughout the White Mountains around 1800, and numerous place names recall her memory. There is a Molledgewock Brook in Errol, a Mollockett Brook near Berlin, and a Molly Lockett Cave near Fryeburg, Maine.

In Conway she is remembered for an incident that occurred while she was bringing some seed corn to Col. McMillan, something she did each spring. This time, however, she laid the sack of corn down by some old logs, and while she was away her corn was taken and ground into meal by mistake. This inspired a local wag to write:

> "Molly Ocket lost her pocket,
> Lydia Fisher found it,
> Lydia carried it to the mill,
> And Uncle Noah ground it."

Even without the corn mishap, however, Molly Ocket would be

remembered in Conway. She once saved the life of a Boston fur trader by warning him of a plot to kill him by an Indian named Tomhegan. To save the trader, Molly Ocket had to make a long journey through the wilderness, but the trader acknowledged and later rewarded her loyalty.

About 1774 she moved to the area of Bethel, Maine, where her name was spelled Mollyockett, but she continued to practice Indian medicine and to perform charitable acts, and citizens of Bethel still observe an annual "Mollyockett Day" in her memory. She died in 1816 and was buried in Andover, Maine, under her Christian name of Mary Agatha.

Monroe, Mt.   5,385 feet   *Southern Peaks*

At the time the Weeks-Brackett party from Lancaster named the peaks of the Presidential Range, James Monroe, the nation's fifth President, was in office, and they named this summit southwest of Mt. Washington for him (see Presidential Range).

M

Monroe, Town   *Connecticut Region*

Hurd's Location was the original name of this town south and west of Littleton, and later it was known as West Lyman, the town then being part of the town of Lyman. Lyman was divided in 1854, and when it became clear that a new name would be needed for the western portion, a dispute arose among area residents. Descendents of John Hurd wanted the town to be named again for him, and they had a strong argument. Hurd had been secretary to Gov. John Wentworth and very active in the affairs of the northern part of the territory. Members of his family were grantees of several nearby towns, including Lyman, Bath, Haverhill, Lisbon, and Whitefield. But another faction wanted the town named after James Monroe, fifth President, who had toured New Hampshire during his term, and the Monroe advocates eventually prevailed.

Montalban Ridge

Moses F. Sweetser, in his White Mountains guide, in 1876 named this long ridge approaching Mt. Washington from the south. The name is simply a Latinization of "White Mountain" (*mons* for "mountain" and *albus* for "white"). It is the New England equivalent of Mont Blanc in the Alps, Craig Eyri in Wales, and Dhaulagiri in the Himalayas.

Monticello Lawn   *Northern Peaks*

On the south shoulder of Mt. Jefferson is a smooth grassy plateau named in 1876 by Moses F. Sweetser in allusion to Thomas Jefferson's home in Virginia.

Moose Brook State Park   *North Country*

The presence of moose at one time on this brook in Gorham doubtless accounts for its name. The name Moose River appeared on Samuel Holland's 1784 map. The region was once known locally as Heath's District.

Moosilauke, Mt.   4,810 feet   *Moosilauke Region*

M As happened so often with place names derived from Indian words, Moosilauke has been spelled literally dozens of ways in its history, with "Moosehillock," "Mooselock," and "Mooselauke" being only a few of the variants. The most common derivation is from two Abenaki words: *moosi* meaning "bald" and *-auke* meaning "place." But other possible translations include "at the place of the ferns," "good moose place along the brook," and "at the smooth place on the summit."

Tradition has it that the Abenaki chief Waternomee ascended the peak in 1685. And Robert Pomeroy, one of Roger's Rangers, is reported to have died on the mountain in 1759. Amos F. Clough, a photographer, and Prof. J. H. Huntington, of the New Hampshire Geological Survey, spent the winter of 1869—70 on the summit of Mt. Moosilauke and thus became pioneers in the field of mountain meteorology.

Moriah, Mt.   4,047 feet
Shelburne, Moriah, Mt.   3,748 feet   *Carter-Moriah Range*

In the Bible, Moriah is identified both as the hill in ancient Palestine on which Abraham prepared to sacrifice Isaac and as the hill in the eastern part of Jerusalem on which Solomon built the Temple. "Moriah" in Hebrew means "provided by Jehovah," and it's thought these mountains south of Gorham received their names from an early settler familiar with these meanings. The name first appeared on Philip Carrigain's map of 1816.

M

Mt. Moriah and Gorham, from *King*.

Moses Rock   *Mahoosuc Range*

In the middle of Shelburne is a huge smooth ledge on the side of what is now known as Mt. Winthrop. And during an early survey, so the story goes, the best lot in town was offered to the man who could first climb this rock. A man named Moses Ingalls (see Ingalls Mt.) thereupon took his shoes off and ran barefoot up the rock. He received, in addition to the lot, the distinction of having the rock named for him.

Muise Mt.   3,610 feet   *North Country*

In 1971 the Groveton Fish and Game Club mounted an effort to have an unnamed peak in the wilderness south of Dixville Notch named for Arthur Muise, a local conservation officer who was very popular. The effort was successful, and officer Muise became probably the only living man in New Hampshire able to enjoy the honor of having a mountain named for him.

N

Nancy in the snow, from *Drake*.

N

Nancy Brook, Cascades, Pond, Mt. 3,906 feet   *Pemigewasset-Carrigain*

A poignant — and true — tale behind the names of these features tells of a young girl named Nancy Barton who was a servant at the estate of Col. Joseph Whipple in Dartmouth, now Jefferson. It would not have been an easy life for the young maid, for Col. Whipple was regarded as a hard master, but while she was at his estate she fell in love with a man tradition says was named Jim Swindell.

Col. Whipple is said to have found out about the romance — and diasapproved — so, on a cold December day in 1778, Col. Whipple arranged for Nancy's lover to be sent to Portsmouth while Nancy was in nearby Lancaster. When Nancy returned and found her lover gone, she fled the estate and pursued him. She got as far as the brook in Crawford Notch that bears her name. There she was later found, frozen in a sitting position, her head resting on her hand and walking cane, her clothing frozen to her body from having walked across the stream.

It's uncertain whether Swindell had left her faithlessly or not, but legend says he was so unsettled by the news of her death that he died shortly after in an insane asylum.

This tale, which is believable at least regarding Col. Whipple, was first printed in Dwight's *Travels* of 1797. A Harvard Latinist once proposed changing the name of Mt. Nancy to Mt. Amoris-gelu — "the Frost of Love" — but fortunately his idea came to naught.

Nash and Sawyer's Location   *Zealand-Twin Mt.*

Benjamin Sawyer and Capt. Timothy Nash were two pioneer settlers who achieved a place in history because of a moose hunt. In April, 1771, Nash was pursuing a moose on what today is called Mitten Mt. (see entry) when he lost his way. He climbed a tree to get his bearings (losing a mitten in doing so and thus naming the mountain) when he spied what appeared to be a notch in the mountains to the south. Nash at the time was a resident of nearby Lunenburg, Vermont, and he knew well what the discovery of a route through the White Mountains would mean to the development of the North Country. He lost no time in exploring the notch and in proving that it did indeed go through the mountains. He carried the news to Gov. John Wentworth, who was also interested and excited. But Gov. Wentworth was cautious too; he had heard other promising but ultimately disappointing tales of the long-sought-after notch, so he agreed to support and reward Nash only if Nash could bring a horse through the notch. (Some versions of the story say the horse was to be laden with rum.)

Nash readily accepted the challenge, and he returned to the North Country where he enlisted the aid of Benjamin Sawyer. It was no easy task they undertook. At one point they had to lower the horse over a cliff with ropes, and it's not recorded whether the rum casks were empty or full when they arrived in Portsmouth.

But arrive they did! And Gov. Wentworth kept his word by giving them in 1773 this strip of land running north from Crawford Notch to slightly beyond Fabyan's. They also received grants in Conway, Lancaster, Bath, and Northumberland, and they sold their grant near Crawford Notch in the same year they received it. Eleazer Rosebrook settled on the site of their grant, and in 1803 the Tenth New Hampshire Turnpike was built through Crawford Notch — thirty-two years after Nash discovered it.

Nathan's Pond   *North Country*

A supposedly true tale of true grit is behind the name of this pond in Stewartstown. Nathan Caswell was an old hunter who camped on the shores of the pond, and one winter day he cut his foot with an axe. Immobilized by the wound and unable to summon any help or expect rescue, he could only watch his provisions dwindle, and he soon faced starvation. One day he heard a dog bark, and taking a gun and crawling toward the sound, he saw a bear in a tree. He shot the bear — no small feat in his condition — and the meat kept him alive until he could try to make his way toward the settlements. He rolled himself in the bear's skin for warmth, but the skin froze, and he had trouble getting free of it. Crawling on his hands and knees, he traveled the last eight miles to help.

Nelson Crag   *Mt. Washington*

In 1870—71 an expedition that included S. A. Nelson of George-town, Massachusetts, spent the winter on Mt. Washington. This was the first party to spend a winter on the mountain, and the overlook on Huntington Ravine from the northeastern shoulder of Mt. Washington was named for Nelson.

New River   *Mt. Washington*

Avalanches and landslides many times have twisted and interrupted this stream draining into the Ellis River from the Gulf of Slides. The river may have broken free from a natural earth dam in 1775, for in that year Jeremy Belknap wrote in his journal that the river "broke forth . . . ; it forms a cascade upwards of 100 feet, visible at its descent into Ellis River." This "newness" of the river would easily explain its name. The river was thrown out of its natural channel in 1776 by an avalanche, but it was put back in again by another avalanche in 1826.

Noon Peak   approx. 2,900 feet   *Waterville Valley* N

Early residents near this peak once used it as a crude sundial, for at midday the sun stood right over it — whence the name.

Northumberland, Town   *North Country*

In 1761 Gov. Benning Wentworth gave this town on the Upper Ammonoosuc River the name Stonington, probably after Stonington, Connecticut. Only ten years later his nephew, Gov. John Wentworth, renamed it Northumberland for Hugh Smithson, Earl Percy and First Duke of Northumberland. The nearby settlement of Percy is named for the same man. Smithson was pro-colonial in the dispute between King George III and the colonies, and his son, James, helped found the new nation's greatest academy of sciences, the Smithsonian Institution, which was named for him.

Notchland   *Montalban Ridge*

In Hart's Location, slightly south of Crawford Notch and on the west side of U. S. Rte. 3, is a stone house now called the Inn Unique, a name it truly deserves. The building was built around 1840 by the Boston dentist Dr. Samuel Bemis who spent his summers in Hart's Location from 1827 to 1840. After building the stone house known as Notchland, Dr. Bemis lived there year round. He came to be known as the "Lord of the Valley," and his life intertwined with that of the colorful Crawford family. He owned a considerable amount of land in the valley, and he was responsible for the naming of many features in the area, including Mt. Crawford, Mt. Resolution, and the Giant's Stairs.

Nowell Ridge   *Northern Peaks*

William G. Nowell was a very active trailbuilder in the White Mountains. He was First Councilor of Improvements for the Appalachian Mountain Club from 1876 to 1878, and he laid out an extensive scheme of path work. He helped Charles E. Lowe cut his path up Mt. Adams in 1875, and the next year Nowell built the first camp on the Northern Peaks. This northwest ridge of Mt. Adams was named for him.

O

The Old Man of the Mountain, from *Bryant*.

Oakes Gulf *Southern Peaks*

William Oakes (1799—1848) first visited the White Mountains while he was a 26-year-old Harvard law student, a trip he made with Charles Pickering, then a young Harvard medical student. Oakes became so engrossed in botany that he dropped law to devote his time to working on the flora of New England, and his beautifully displayed specimens were widely distributed. In 1848 he published the *Scenery of the White Mountains*, with illustrations by Godfrey N. Frankenstein and Isaac Sprague, and he was planning a guide book when he met an untimely death by falling from a ferryboat in Boston Harbor. This gulf southeast of Mt. Monroe was named for him by Prof. Edward Tuckerman, a fellow botanist.

O

Odell, Town *North Country*

The unincorporated town of Odell, comprising nearly 24,000 acres east of Stratford, was granted in 1834 to Richard Odell of Conway for $1,863. In 1940 the town had eighty-two residents, but by 1960 it had none.

The Old Man of the Mountain *Franconia-Garfield*

The origin of the name of this rock prominence on Cannon Mt., also called Profile Mt., is self-evident. The Old Man is both the official and unofficial symbol of New Hampshire, and each year thousands of persons travel through Franconia Notch to view the face made famous by the short story by Nathaniel Hawthorne. Daniel Webster, a native son of New Hampshire, once said: "Men hang out signs indicative of their respective trades. Shoemakers hang out a gigantic shoe; jewelers a monster watch; and the dentist hangs out a gold tooth. But in the mountains of New Hampshire, God Almighty has hung out a sign to show that there He makes men."

Old Mast Road   *Chocorua Region*

   The Old Mast Road runs between Mt. Wonalancet and Mts. Mexico and Paugus. It is said to have been built for hauling out the tallest white pine logs to serve as masts for ships of the king's navy in colonial days.

Old Shag Camp   *Chocorua Region*

   "Old Shag" was an early name for Mt. Paugus, whence the name for this camp just below the summit ledges on the eastern side.

Oliverian Brook, Notch   *Chocorua Region*

   The name Oliverian Brook appeared on maps as early as 1776. It is said to be derived from a man named Oliver falling into the brook named for him.

O

Ore Hill   *Cannon-Kinsman*

   Iron was discovered on this hill in Sugar Hill in 1805, and mining operations flourished until 1850, when competition from the West made the mines unprofitable.

Oscar, Mt.   2,748 feet   *Zealand-Twin Mt.*

   Southwest of Fabyan's is this low mountain, named for Oscar G. Barron, for many years manager of the Fabyan House.

Osceola, Mt.   4,326 feet   *Waterville Valley*

   The meaning of the name of this peak south of Kancamagus Pass is known, but not how it got there. Osceola has nothing to do with any New Hampshire Indians, referring instead to the Seminole chief in the Florida Everglades who led his people in stubborn resistance against the whites and was finally captured in Georgia in 1837. The name itself is derived from the Seminole *asi-yaholo*, meaning literally "black drink" but also referring to a ceremonial potion. Nathaniel L. Goodrich, in his history of Waterville Valley, suggests that both Mt. Tecumseh and Mt. Osceola were named by E. J. Connable of Jackson, Michigan, who came to Waterville Valley in 1859 and built the present Patton Cottage.

Osgood Path, Ridge   *Northern Peaks*

Benjamin F. Osgood was a famous guide at the Glen House in the late 1800's, and in 1878 he with others opened the path leading from the Glen House to Mt. Madison. This path, and the ridge it follows, were named for him. Though a portion of the lower end of the path has since been relocated, the remaining sections of trail are the oldest route still in use to the summit of Mt. Madison.

Owl's Head   *Pemigewasset-Carrigain*

There are at least three Owl's Heads in the White Mountains: one forming the north peak of Cherry Mt.; one between Potter's Pond and the Percy Peaks near Stratford; and one east of Franconia Ridge. All received their names most likely because of their shapes. The Owl's Head on Cherry Mt. was at one time called Mt. Martha.

Chief Passaconaway, from *Beals*.

P_Q

Page Hill

Mahoosuc Range

A hunter named "Yager" Page made a large clearing near this mountain in the town of Success in the early 1800's, and about 1823 there was a log cabin at the site, the only house in the town. Five families dwelt there. Page Hill is a name that occurs also in Lancaster and Tamworth.

Passaconaway, Mt.   4,060 feet

Chocorua Region

P

In the language of the Penacook Indians, the name Passaconaway was really *papisse-conwa*, and it meant "papoose bear" or "bear cub." But there was nothing cublike about the Passaconaway history remembers. Passaconaway became chief of the Penacooks in 1620, and under his leadership the Penacooks ruled a powerful federation of tribes living mostly in what is now New Hampshire. War, famine, and pestilence had decimated the Indians a few years prior to Passaconaway's succession, but the tribes still numbered thirteen, according to some estimates, and their leader became an almost legendary figure. Legend says, for example, that at the moment of his death he "translated" to heaven from the summit of Mt. Washington in a sled drawn by wolves. Legend also says that just before his death, Passaconaway warned his fellow Indians not to quarrel with their English neighbors or they would be destroyed in the ensuing conflict; his son, Wonalancet, and his grandson, Kancamagus, are said to have heeded his words.

The mountain north of Whiteface bearing his name was once known as North Whiteface. The name Passaconaway was once applied to the mountain now known as Tripyramid.

Paugus Brook, Pass, Mt.   3,200 feet

Chocorua Region

On May 8, 1725, Capt. John Lovewell led a party of thirty-four men from Dunstable, Massachusetts, in an attack on an Indian village at the head of a pond near what is now Fryeburg. The Indians were Pequakets, natives of the region, and they were led by their under-chief, Paugus. The battle has been called Lovewell's Massacre, and justly so, for in it about sixty Indians and eighteen whites were killed, including both Lovewell and Paugus. Legend tells that during the battle Paugus and a white militiaman had sighted each other and begun scrambling to load their guns. They both shot at the same time — and both missed! Paugus, hastily priming his weapon, yelled, "Me kill you!" The white had a self-priming rifle, and he struck the weapon on the ground with such force that it self-primed. "The chief lies!" the man shouted back, and shot him dead.

Paugus Mt., an irregular mass west of Mt. Chocorua, was once called Old Shag because of the many ledges on it. The *History of Carroll County* says other names for Mt. Paugus have included Hunchback, Deer, Frog, Middle, Berry, and Bald. The present name was suggested by Lucy Larcom, a young poet who was a summer visitor in the White Mountains and a friend of John Greenleaf Whittier.

P

Peabody River and Mt. Madison, from *King*.

Peabody River   *Carter-Moriah Range*

Early guidebooks tell the story of a Mr. Peabody of Andover, Maine. He was passing the night in an Indian cabin at the height of land between the Saco and Androscoggin watersheds when suddenly he and the Indians were aroused from sleep by a roaring nearby. They escaped from the cabin just in time to watch it being swept away by a torrent that had sprung from the hillside. A natural dam had doubtless given way. The name is old, appearing on Samuel Holland's map of 1784.

Pearl Lake   *Cannon-Kinsman*

Originally, this pond near Lisbon was called Bear Pond, because of the numerous bears there. Then it was called Mink Pond, for the numerous mink there. And finally it was called Pearl Pond — for the pearls. In the summer of 1854 some fishermen discovered in some clamshells "some substances which imagination easily manufactured in pearls." Rumor spread that a man named True Page found a pearl worth $30, and a "pearl rush" was on. Piles of discarded clamshells began to grow on the shore, and for days between fifty and seventy-five people could be seen knee-deep in the pond's water, looking for the pearl-bearing clams. They found few, if any.

P

Peboamauk Cascade   *North Country*

In Abenaki *peboamauk* translates to mean "wintry place," or "winter's home," and the name is appropriate for these falls. They are located on the southeast side of the Crescent Range in Ice Gulch, a deep cut in the mountain that receives little sunlight and thereby remains cool enough to allow ice to exist there even in summer.

Pemigewasset, Mt.   2,554 feet   *Cannon-Kinsman*

This mountain on the east side of Franconia Notch has a double association with Indians. The mountain takes its name from the Pemigewasset River to the south, whose name is derived from an Abenaki word meaning "swift current" or "rapids." But the mountain also has on its northwest shoulder the famous Indian Head, a natural rock formation that resembles the profile of an Indian. The name Pemigewasset Mt. first appeared on a map prepared for Eastman's *White Mountain Guide* of 1863.

Pemigewasset River   *Pemigewasset-Carrigain*

Affectionately called "the Pemi" by hikers, the Pemigewasset River takes its name from a tribe of Indians that once lived in the river valley. The Indian word was *pamijowasik,* and in Abenaki it meant "swift, extended current" or "rapids." The East Branch of the Pemigewasset was called Merrimack by mapmaker Phillip Carrigain in 1816. A map printed in 1767 called the river the Pemijawsitts River.

Pequawket Pond   *Conway-Bartlett-Jackson*

The Pequakets were a tribe of Indians that lived in the region that included this pond two miles west of Conway (see Conway). The Indian word *pe-que-auk-et* has been variously translated to mean "clear valley lands bordering a crooked stream" and "broken land." Pequawket was an early name for Conway.

P

The Perch   *Northern Peaks*

At an elevation of 4,300 feet and "perched" on the northeast slope of Mt. Adams, this camp was the highest of three built by the noted White Mountains trailmaker J. Rayner Edmands. It was named by him in 1892.

Percy Village, Pond, Peaks   3,418 and 3,220 feet   *North Country*

The Percy Peaks, twin sugarloaf-shaped summits north of Groveton, took their names from the nearby village of Percy, once much larger than the present tiny settlement. The village was named for Hugh Smithson, Earl Percy and First Duke of Northumberland (1715—1786). The nearby town of Northumberland was named for the same man. The English nobleman was a friend of the American colonies and argued against the policies of King George III. The Percy Peaks and Percy Pond appeared on Philip Carrigain's map of 1816.

Phillips Brook   *North Country*

Old residents of the area say this brook, a tributary of the Upper

Ammonoosuc River, derives its name froim King Philip, an Indian chief who sold most of northern New Hampshire to three white men. The *History of Stark*, however, gives as the origin a Mr. Phillips who, along with a man named Francis Lang, moved to the area from Saco, Maine, and built the first mill on the brook in the 1820's. Neither explanation has received corroboration from other records or informants, although Phillips Brook appeared on Philip Carrigain's 1816 map, suggesting that the name predated the arrival of Mr. Phillips.

Pickering, Mt.   1,945 feet   *Montalban Ridge*

The name Pickering Mt. first appeared on Hithcock's 1876 map, and it commemorates a family long devoted to the White Mountains. Charles Pickering (1805—1878) was, among other things, a naturalist, and in 1838—42 he was chief zoologist on the U. S. exploring expedition to the Antarctic and the northwest coast of America. He was twenty when he first climbed Mt. Washington in 1825 with William Oakes, and he continued to explore the White Mountains with enthusiasm for many years, often with his close friend Prof. W. D. Peck.

P

The love of the mountains continued in his nephews Edward Charles Pickering (1846—1919) and Edward's brother, William Henry Pickering (1858—1938), both noted astronomers. Several features in the White Mountains were named by William Pickering, and to E. Charles Pickering belongs an additional achievement. He had been exploring the mountains for several years, and he enjoyed the company of persons who shared his interests. So, on Jan. 1, 1876, E. Charles Pickering, then Thayer Professor of Physics at the Massachusetts Institute of Technology, formally invited fifty persons to a meeting of "those interested in mountain exploration." Prof. Charles E. Fay was chairman of this preliminary meeting, which was held at MIT on Jan. 8. The first regular meeting was held on Feb. 9, when a permanent organization was formed. There were thirty-nine charter members, and E. Charles Pickering was chosen the group's first president. The club was the Appalachian Mountain Club (AMC).

Today the AMC has thousands of members, and no other organization has had such an intimate and constructive association with the White Mountains. Its members have built trails, huts, and shelters; they have studied the mountains and written guides to their exploration and enjoyment; and most important they have constantly endeavored to keep the White Mountains the kind of wild natural area that the Pickerings found so exciting over a hundred years ago.

Pierce, Mt.   4,312 feet   *Southern Peaks*

Only time will tell which of two "official" names of this peak will ultimately survive, if either. The peak east of Crawford Notch was originally called Mt. Clinton (see entry) after Gov. DeWitt Clinton of New York (1769—1828), but in 1913 the name was changed by the New Hampshire Legislature to Mt. Pierce. The lawmakers wanted to honor Franklin Pierce, fourteenth President and the "only citizen or resident of New Hampshire who has been the incumbent of that exalted office." Mapmakers and hikers, however, ignored the change, and in 1915 the Committee on Nomenclature of the Appalachian Mountain Club recommended using the old name on AMC maps.

P

Piermont, Town   *Connecticut Region*

The origin of the name of this town on the Connecticut River is obscure. It has been suggested that the name is a corruption of "piedmont," a geographical term referring to a plain lying near a mountain range, and Piermont, in some respects, does indeed resemble a piedmont. But no firm evidence exists supporting this as the origin of the name, and without such evidence the true origin of the name must be said to be unknown.

Pike Village   *Connecticut Region*

Located in southern Haverhill, this tiny village owes its name to Alonzo Pike, who had the good fortune of being shown an immense rock bed of "Bethlehem gneiss" by the New Hampshire State Geologist, Prof. Charles Hitchcock. The stone made excellent sharpening stones, and throughout the world tool grinders and sharpeners produced in northern New Hampshire were known as "Pikestones." The Alonzo Pike Company was formed in 1860, and at one time no fewer than sixteen members of the Pike family lived in the village, most of them working for the company. A declining market and exhaustion of the mineral deposit meant the eventual end for the business, though the village, where many houses were built by the company, survives.

Pike Pond   *North Country*

People, not pickerel, were responsible for the name of this pond located north of the village of Percy on the Upper Ammonoosuc River. The pond was named for its first owners, the Pike family.

Pilot Range, Mt.   3,710 feet   *North Country*

Far-ranging hunters and scouts journeying along the upper Connecticut River used these mountains as landmarks, and they called them the "Land Pilot Hills." This name was in use as early as 1814, though the town plan of Percy, made about 1803, refers to "Land of Pilot Mt." and doubtless refers to Mt. Pilot, the second highest peak in the range (see Mt. Hutchins). Mt. Cabot, 4,180 feet, is the highest. Local legend says the name Mt. Pilot is derived from the name of the dog of Jonathan Willard, an eccentric recluse who lived in the wilderness near the notch that now bears his name, but the prior history of the name Land Pilot Mt. makes this theory untenable. The Pilot Range was called Little Moosehillock by Timothy Dwight, who passed through the region in 1797 and again in 1803.

P

Pine Mt.   2,404 feet   *Northern Peaks*

Once called both Camel's Hump and Camel's Rump, this mountain in Randolph takes its present name from the fine stands of pines that stood on the mountain before fires destroyed most of them.

Pinkham Grant, Notch   *Mt. Washington*

The resourcefulness and hardiness of the early settlers of the White Mountains are nowhere better illustrated than in the lives of Capt. Joseph Pinkham and his son Daniel. The captain, his wife, and four children left Madbury, New Hampshire, to homestead in what is now Jackson, which at that time was called, not surprisingly, New Madbury. They arrived April 6, 1789, and here is how Joseph later recalled their arrival at the homestead to his son Daniel, who in 1789 would have been ten years old:

"The snow was five feet deep on the level. There was no road to

Bartlett, and we traveled on the snow. Our provisions, furniture, and clothing were on a handsled, to which the boys had harnessed the hog, their only animal, and he did efficient service. On arriving at our home we found the log house erected the previous autumn half-buried in snow, and had to shovel a way through to find the door. The house had no chimney, no stove, no floor, no window, except the open door, or the smoke-hole in the roof. We built a fireplace at one end of green logs and replaced them as often as they burned out, until the snow left us so that we could get rocks to supply their place. We had but two chairs and one bedstead. Thus we lived until summer, when we moved the balance of our furniture from Conway. There was much poverty here at this early period, and the means of living scarce. A few families had cows, and could afford the luxury of milk porridge, but many were obliged to make their porridge of meal and water only. The rivers afforded trout, and these constituted a large portion of our food. They were dried in the sun and roasted by the fire, and eaten usually without salt, as that was a scarce article in the new settlement."

P Daniel grew up on the family homestead in Jackson, and later he built a blacksmith shop there. Although Daniel never formally learned any trade, he became a blacksmith, a mason, a carpenter, a wheelwright, and even a dentist. But his subsequent fame rests on his attempts to be a roadbuilder. Under an agreement with the State of New Hampshire, Daniel was to build a road through the notch that would connect Jackson with Gorham. His father Joseph had begun such a road in 1789. Daniel was given three years to complete the task, and if he succeeded he was to receive a tract of land one-half mile wide on each side of the road from Jackson to Gorham, as well as all the state lands in the town of Jackson. But the road would be twelve miles long, through a nightmare of boulders, streams, dense timber, and steep, rugged terrain.

Two years later Daniel Pinkham had his road nearly completed, but heavy rains in August, 1826, caused huge landslides that destroyed much of his progress. He abandoned the project.

Later, he did construct a toll road through the notch, but deep snows discouraged travel, and this project, too, was not a financial success for him.

In 1829, at the age of fifty, Daniel Pinkham moved his family from Jackson to Pinkham's Grant and homesteaded anew. He lived there for six years. Finally, in 1834, after ten years of toil, disappointment, and poverty, his grant was confirmed, and in the speculations of 1835—36 he sold enough land to enable him to buy a farm in Lancaster. There he died in June, 1855.

Pinkham Notch was known by that name as early as 1851. Before that it was known as Pinkham Woods and before that as Eastern Pass.

Piper Trail   *Chocorua Region*

Joshua Piper was one of the "Piper Boys" who ran a stagecoach near Mt. Chocorua, and he cut the first trail up the mountain. He later used the trail in guiding hiking parties up the mountain and also on bear hunts.

Pittsburg, Town   *North Country*

Pittsburg is unique, not so much in being the largest and northernmost town in New Hampshire, but in being a town that once was also an independent nation (see Indian Stream). But while Pittsburg's history and geography may be unique, its name is not. Pittsfield, New Hampshire, and all the other Pittsburgs in the U. S. are named after the same man, William Pitt (1708—1778), the great English statesman and advocate of mild treatment for the American colonies.

P

Pleasant, Mt.   4,761 feet   *Southern Peaks*

According to the White Mountains explorer Prof. Edward Tuckerman, this peak in the southern Presidential Range was called Dome Mt. in 1820. In July of that year, the Weeks-Brackett party (see Presidential Range) named it Mt. Pleasant, and the U. S. Geological Survey later called it Pleasant Dome. In 1824, in the *American Journal of Science*, James Pierce called it Mt. Prospect. Today it is called Mt. Eisenhower (see entry).

Pliny Range   *North Country*

Pliny, as every Latin student knows, was a first century Roman poet, and like so many other eponymous figures in White Mountains history, a great student of botany. It's said the name was given to this range in the southern part of the Kilkenny Basin by a local gentleman who had some acquaintance with classical history.

Pond of Safety   *North Country*

James Rider, Benjamin Hicks, William Danforth, and Lazarus Homes were soldiers in the Continental Army who had been captured by the British and later paroled. American officers believed the soldiers' parole papers were spurious, and they ordered the men back into the ranks. The four refused to break their word to the British and to bear arms against them, so they returned to their native town of Jefferson in the White Mountains. They were branded as deserters by the Army, so they fled to this wilderness pond in the easterly section of Randolph (then called Durand) where they lived for the next three years until the war was over. They then returned to Jefferson where they became prominent and respected citizens. In 1826 they were exonerated of the desertion charge, and their names were added to the Army's pension lists.

Pondicherry Notch   *Zealand-Twin Mt.*

P Around 1907 John Anderson of the Mt. Crawford House suggested this name for the notch between Mt. Deception and Cherry Mt. because Pondicherry was the original name for Cherry Mt. The name Pondicherry is quite old; it appeared on the charter map of Bretton Woods, which was granted in 1772, and in the journal of Jeremy Belknap, who toured the region in 1784. But of the origin of the name, little is known. It is possible the name describes a pond around which cherries grew, and it has also been suggested that the name was given by French explorers who were recalling Pondicherry, capital of French India and the site of frequent struggles between the French and the British.

Pontook Reservoir   *North Country*

The name Pontook is an abbreviation of the Abenaki word *pontoocook*, mening "falls in the river," and indeed there are falls just below these wetlands on the Androscoggin River above Berlin.

Potato Hill   *Pemigewasset-Carrigain*

Early settlers grew California potatoes on this hill near Elbow Lake in Woodstock and sold them to Elder Rope's Starch Mill on Glover Brook.

Presidential Range   *Mt. Washington*

On July 31, 1820, a party of seven ascended Mt. Washington for the

Presidential Range from Jefferson, from *King*.

P

stated purpose of naming the high peaks. The seven were Adino N. Brackett, John W. Weeks, General John Wilson, Charles J. Stuart, N. S. Dennison, Samuel A. Pearsons — all of Lancaster — and the mapmaker Philip Carrigain. They were guided in their journey by Ethan Allen Crawford.

Mt. Washington had already received its name, so they decided to christen the adjacent peaks for the four subsequent Presidents — John Adams, Thomas Jefferson, James Madison, and James Monroe, who was in office at the time. The naming was a momentous event, and the namers had brought with them plenty of "O-be-joyful" so that proper toasts could be drunk. Then, running out of Presidents, they christened Mt. Franklin for Benjamin Franklin, and the next peak to the southwest they called Mt. Pleasant (now Mt. Eisenhower), a name it facetiously has been suggested was inspired by the O-be-joyful.

Since then the names of other Presidents have been added to the Presidential Range — John Quincy Adams, Franklin Pierce, and most recently Dwight David Eisenhower. Other Presidents having their names on peaks in the White Mountains, though not in the Presidential Range, are Abraham Lincoln, James A. Garfield, Grover Cleveland, and Calvin Coolidge.

Profile Lake   *Cannon-Kinsman*

It is said the Indians rarely visited this lake because they feared the reflection of the stern visage above. Early settlers called the pond Ferrin Pond, after the Ferrin family who helped build a road through Franconia Notch. It was also called Old Man's Washbowl, for the Old Man of the Mountain. Today the pond is called Profile Lake, corresponding to Profile Mt. above it.

Profile Mt.   4,077 feet   *Cannon-Kinsman*

As early as 1827 this mountain was called Profile Mt., but it has also borne other names — Jackson Mt., Freak Mt., and Cannon Mt., the last name widely used today. The name was officially changed to Profile Mt. in 1927 following the successful effort by the Rev. Guy Roberts of Whitefield to preserve the famous stone face. Apparently Roberts unearthed the old name while doing research during his campaign.

P
Q

Prospect, Mt.   2,059 feet   *North Country*

Early residents of Lancaster called this knob south of the village Mt. Prospect because of the extended views from its top. John Wingate Weeks (1860—1920), U. S. Secretary of War during President Harding's administration, built a summer home atop the mountain, and the family later gave the home and the mountain to New Hampshire to become Weeks State Park. John W. Weeks was largely responsible for the creation of the White Mountain National Forest.

Pulpit Rock   *Carter-Moriah Range*

On the east side of Carter Dome is a huge boulder named Pulpit Rock because it is partly detached from the cliff and is evocative of a pulpit.

Quimby's Pillow   *Carter-Moriah Range*

In 1879 Prof. E. T. Quimby occupied the summit of Mt. Moriah as one of the stations of the U. S. Coast and Geodetic Survey, and this boulder, weighing about 500 pounds and located three-quarters of a mile from the summit, was jocularly named for him.

R

Robert Rogers, from *Drake*.

R

Randolph, Town, Path, Mt.   3,090 feet   *Northern Peaks*

The town of Randolph was originally chartered in 1772 as Durand, named for an Englsih business associate of Gov. Benning Wentworth. The name was changed to Randolph in 1824 by Gov. Levi Woodbury to honor his friend, Congressman John Randolph of Virginia (1773—1833). Known as John Randolph of Roanoke, he was a descendent of Pocahontas. He later became a U. S. Senator and a leading advocate of states' rights.

The Randolph Path, which goes from Dolly Copp Road over the slopes of Mts. Madison and Adams to join the Gulfside Trail in Edmands Col, was built by the famous White Mountains trailmaker J. Rayner Edmands. He constructed the portion above the timberline in 1893 and the sections below timberline in 1897—99.

Randolph Mt. was originally called Black Mt., but it appeared on an 1858 map under its present name.

Rattlesnake Mt.   1,550 feet   *Conway-Bartlett-Jackson*

New Hampshire does have rattlesnakes — though they are very rare as far north as Conway — and consequently New Hampshire has several Rattlesnake Mts. This peak in the Green Hills east of North Conway is one of them. There is also a Rattlesnake Mt. near Keewaydin Lake in the Maine portion of the White Mountains.

Raymond Cataract, Path   *Mt. Washington*

In 1859 Major Curtis B. Raymond, a veteran mountaineer, led an exploring party to these falls, and his companions named them in his honor. Four years later Major Raymond blazed a path nearby to connect the Carriage Road with the Tuckerman Ravine Path. He completed the path that now bears his name in 1879, and he maintained it until his death in 1893 when his widow generously continued to maintain it.

Redstone   *Conway-Bartlett-Jackson*

In 1886 quarry operations were begun at this site between Conway and North Conway, the object being the red granite located there. A small industrial settlement grew up, taking its name from the color of the granite.

Resolution, Mt.   3,428 feet   *Montalban Ridge*

Nathaniel T. B. Davis was son-in-law of Abel Crawford and manager of the Mt. Crawford House in Crawford Notch. In the 1840's he set about building the third bridle path to Mt. Washington, but he got only as far as this mountain before he gave up discouraged, something easily understandable given the rugged terrain. Later, however, and with new determination and resolution, he tried again and this time succeeded, so Dr. Samuel Bemis, a friend and neighbor, suggested this name for the mountain where Davis started the second time.

R

Ripley Falls   *Pemigewasset-Carrigain*

In 1858 an old fisherman reported to Henry W. Ripley of North Conway that he had seen a wonderful cascade on what was then called Cow Brook, at the southern end of Crawford Notch. Ripley and a friend followed up on the report, which they discovered to be true. In the process they also renamed Cow Brook, calling it instead Avalanche Brook because it flows near the track of the landslide that wiped out the Willey family in 1826. The falls were named for Ripley at the suggestion of the Rev. Thomas Starr King.

Only a few persons have ever equalled Ripley's familiarity with and love for the White Mountains. Born in Fryeburg, Maine, in 1828, he began visiting the White Mountains when he was seven years old; the summer of 1889 was his fifty-third consecutive visit to the White Mountains, and he had climbed Mt. Washington, in summer and in winter, eighty-five times. He was well-known for his conversation and writing about the White Mountains.

Riverton   *North Country*

Named doubtless because of its location on the Israel River in Jefferson, this tiny settlement was the birthplace of Thaddeus Lowe (1832-1913), an aeronautic scientist and early student of the atmosphere.

Rogers Ledge   *North Country*

The present name of this rock outcropping in the Kilkenny Basin is the result of a crusade. The ledge previously had been known as Nigger Nose, but in 1955 the Right Reverend Robert McConnell Hatch, Bishop of the Episcopal Diocese of Western Massachusetts and a long-time summer resident of Randolph, decided it should be changed. He proposed the name Rogers Ledge to honor Major Robert Rogers, who led the famous Rogers Rangers during the French and Indian Wars. Hatch pointed out that though Major Rogers ended the Indian raids in the North Country and made the region safe for settlement, no geographical feature there was named for him.

Hatch discovered that Edward DeCourcy, a highly respected New Hampshire weekly newspaper editor, had written an editorial suggesting that the name Nigger Nose be changed, and the two worked together to accomplish this. Their cause was joined by the Automobile Legal Association, which in 1964 wrote to U. S. Secretary of the Inerior Stewart Udall that the name Nigger Nose "offends the sensibilities of all right-thinking people." The association advocated naming the ledge after the late President Kennedy.

Their efforts were successful — though Major Rogers won out over President Kennedy — and in 1964 the U. S. Board on Geographic Names in the U. S. Dept. of the Interior formally decreed that henceforth the outcrop would be known as Rogers Ledge.

R

Rollins Trail   *Chocorua Region*

Dr. William H. Rollins, who had a summer home in Tamworth for many years, in 1899 paid for the construction of this path connecting Mts. Passaconaway and Whiteface.

Rosebrook Range, Mt.   3,007 feet   *Zealand-Twin Mt.*

Capt. Eleazer Rosebrook was an early guide and settler in the White Mountains. In 1792 he followed his son-in-law Abel Crawford in settling the site later known as Fabyan's. (Abel Crawford moved down the road twelve miles.) In 1803 the New Hampshire Legislature authorized the construction of a turnpike through Crawford Notch, and as travel and business increased, Capt. Rosebrook built a large two-story dwelling abutting a mound known as the "Giant's Grave." This inn built by Rosebrook has been called the first summer hotel in the White Mountains. Rosebrook's daughter married Abel Crawford, and in 1817

Rosebrook gave his inn to his grandson Ethan Allen Crawford, who along with Ethan's future bride, Lucy, nursed Rosebrook during a long illness.

The Rosebrook Range, an extension of the Willey Range, includes Mts. Echo (3,084 feet), Rosebrook (3,007 feet), and Oscar (2,748 feet).

Round, Mt. 3,890 feet   *North Country*

Its appearance from the west is most likely responsible for the name of this peak in the Pliny Range.

Royce, Mt. 3,202 feet   *Chatham Region*

R

Capt. Vere Royse was a soldier and surveyor and at one time served as surveyor-general of the Province of New Hampshire. He made the charter maps for many towns in the White Mountains, including Chatham, Bartlett, and Bretton Woods. In 1769 he was granted 2,000 acres near the Saco River between Glen and Bartlett; the land was given for his services "during the late war in North America." This peak west of Evans Notch, and nearby East Royce Mt. in Maine (3,115 feet), are named for him. The name Royse Mt. appeared on Samuel Holland's 1784 map.

S

Silver Cascade, from *King*.

S

Sabattus Mt.   1,280 feet   *Chatham Region*

Sabattus was a Pequaket Indian living near Conway. The name Sabbattus may have been a corruption of St. Jean Baptiste, a name given to the Indian by the French. Sabattus was killed in a quarrel at Boscawen in 1753.

Sabbaday Brook, Falls   *Chocorua Region*

According to tradition, early settlers on their way to new homes paused on the Sabbath Day near this brook north of Mt. Tripyramid. They pondered the likely conditions at their destination, reconsidered their venture, and turned around.

Sable, Mt.   3,504 feet   *Chatham Region*

The name of this summit in northwestern Chatham appeared on Philip Carrigain's map of 1816. The name could refer to the peak being dark in color. Or it could refer to the peak at one time having mink on it. Or it could refer to something else entirely. No information has been found as to the origin of this name.

Sachem Peak   3,060 feet   *Waterville Valley*

Sachem meant "chief" to the Indians of the Northeast, and this peak was named by Prof. C. E. Fay perhaps because it is the highest peak in the Acteon Ridge.

Saco River   *Conway-Bartlett-Jackson*

Saco in the Abenaki language meant "flowing out" or "outlet," and the Abenaki-speaking people that came to live along the Saco River from its headwaters at tiny Saco Lake in Crawford Notch to its mouth on the Atlantic were known as the Sokosis. Before white settlement, the Sokosis lived near the islands at the mouth of the Saco, whence the name meaning "outlet." But the Sokosis later came to inhabit the entire reach of the river, becoming known as Ossipees and Pequakets according to where they settled.

Saddleback Mt.   3,812 feet   *Mahoosuc Range*

The shape of this mountain east of Grafton Notch is the origin of its name. The mountain has also been called Bear River Whitecap and, more commonly, Baldpate.

S

Salmacis Falls   *Northern Peaks*

On July 21, 1879, according to a contemporary account in *Among the Clouds*, some visitors from Randolph named these falls on Snyder Brook for the wood nymph, Salmacis. In classical mythology, however, Salmacis was a fountain in Caria that rendered effeminate all who bathed in it, and it was in this fountain that Hermaphroditus changed his sex.

Salmon Hole Brook   *Cannon-Kinsman*

On the Ammonoosuc River two and a half miles south of Lisbon is a deep hole where salmon weighing as much as twenty-five pounds once were caught. The Indians salted them for the winter, and the white settlers also fed on them until industrial mills upstream polluted the water and destroyed the fishing.

Sanguinari, Mt.   2,748 feet   *North Country*

Sanguinarius in Latin means "of the color of blood," and this peak forming the north flank of Dixville Notch was named for the brilliant blood-red color of its rocks at sunset.

Sargent's Purchase   *Mt. Washington*

In 1831, these lands that include the summit of Mt. Washington, as well as Lakes of the Clouds, Tuckerman Ravine, and Mt. Monroe, were purchased for $300 by a group of men among whom was Jacob Sargent of Thornton, New Hampshire.

Saunders, Mt.   3,120 feet   *Pemigewasset-Carrigain*

The Saunders family for generations owned and managed timberlands in Livermore, and one of its members, Charles C. Saunders of Lawrence, Massachusetts, gained recognition as an early promoter of scientific forestry, as well as being a charter member of the Appalachian Mountain Club. Local people had long called this mountain, between Mt. Nancy and Livermore Station, Mt. Saunders, and the name was formally approved by the Committee on Nomenclature of the AMC in 1915. The name honors the Hon. Daniel Saunders, who died at Lawrence in 1917 at the age of ninety-four.

S

Sawyer Pond, Rock, River   *Conway-Bartlett-Jackson*

Benjamin Sawyer was an early settler and explorer in the White Mountains who, along with Timothy Nash (see Nash and Sawyer's Location), achieved a place in history by helping prove that men and horses could travel through Crawford Notch. The two accomplished their goal only with the greatest difficulty, and several times they had to lower the horse down rock faces with ropes. Finally, says tradition, just as they had overcome their last obstacle, they halted and celebrated by breaking a bottle — presumably of rum — on Sawyer Rock in commemoration of their victory.

Scar Ridge   *Waterville Valley*

Running northwest from Mt. Osceola, this ridge was named in 1876 by Prof. F. W. Clarke and Gaetano Lanza, who made an early ascent of it. The name is derived from the ridge having recently been scarred by landslides at the time of its naming.

The Scaur   *Waterville Valley*

   Scaur is just a variant spelling of *scar*. The Scaur is a rock outlook
between Mad River and Slide Brook.

Screw Auger Falls   *Mahoosuc Range*

   On the Bear River, southwest of Grafton Notch, rushing water has
worn holes into the solid rock of the river's bed. So regular are some of
the holes that they look as though they had been made with an auger,
whence the name.

Second College Grant   *North Country*

S   This tract of uninhabited forest land in the far north of New
Hampshire was Gov. Benning Wentworth's second choice — whence
the name — as a site for Dartmouth College. His first choice was the
present Town of Landaff, and his third was Hanover, the present site.
Six square miles of land here were officially granted to the college in
1807, and Dartmouth enjoyed considerable revenue from subsequent
sales of real estate and timber. An act of the legislature in 1919 authorized
the continued use of the name Second College Grant in the list of state
towns and gave to the college whatever state money and resources
Second College Grant might be allocated.

Shaw, Mt.   2,566 feet   *Conway-Bartlett-Jackson*

   Lemuel Shaw was a member of Dr. Jacob Bigelow's botanical
expedition to the White Mountains in 1816, the first to explore Mt.
Washington for scientific knowledge. Shaw was later a chief justice of
Massachusetts. This peak northeast of Mt. Kearsarge North was named
for him.

Camp Shehadi   *Waterville Valley*

   In 1899 the Wonalancet Outdoor Club used the proceeds from a
lecture to build the predecessor of this camp located one-fifth mile from
the summit of Mt. Whiteface. The lecturer was one Shehadi Abdullah
Shehadi. (The original shelter was replaced in 1930.)

Shelburne, Town   *Mahoosuc Range*

In 1769 this town straddling the Androscoggin River was named for William Petty Fitzmaurice (1737-1805), Earl of Shelburne. He was one of the American colonies' staunchest friends in Parliament in the days before the American Revolution.

Short Line Trail   *Northern Peaks*

The well-known White Mountains trailmaker J. Rayner Edmands in 1899—1901 constructed this path to connect the Air Line Trail with the King Ravine Trail. It was named for its short length.

Silver Cascade   *Southern Peaks*

S

On the west side of Mt. Jackson, flowing into the Saco River, are a series of falls known as Silver Cascade. The name has been in general use since the 1850's when the Rev. Thomas Starr King visited the area. Before that they were known as the Second Flume, probably because it is south of Flume Cascade.

Silver Spring, Mt.   2,995 feet   *Conway-Bartlett-Jackson*

On some maps this peak southwest of Bartlett is called Bartlett Haystack, a name derived from the peak's shape. The peak has also been called Revelation.

Six Husbands Trail   *Great Gulf*

Weetamoo was a queen of the Penacook Indians who, according to tradition, had six husbands in succession. She was the heroine of John Greenleaf Whittier's poem "The Bridal of Pennacook," and, when the Great Gulf Trail was blazed in 1908, these beautiful falls below Spaulding Lake were named for her. (Weetamoo Mt. was also named for her.) The next year, the section of the trail connecting the Great Gulf with the Gulfside Trail was constructed, and it was named for Weetamoo's six husbands. The name was later applied to the entire trail.

S

Snow Arch, Tuckerman
Ravine, from *Drake*.

Skookumchuck Brook   *Franconia-Garfield*

This name is analogous to a glacial "erratic," appearing out of
context far from its original place of origin. The name is derived from
jargon of the Chinook Indians of the Pacific Northwest, and it means
"dashing water" or "rapids."

Slope Mt.   2,008 feet   *Chatham Region*

The derivation of the name of this mountain northwest of Chatham is unknown, but it appeared as Sloop Mt. on Samuel Holland's map of 1784.

Snow Arch   *Mt. Washington*

Hikers have been fascinated by this natural arch of snow in Tuckerman Ravine at least since 1829, when Ethan Allen Crawford guided a party of botanists into the region. During the winter, snow blows over the steep walls of the ravine and accumulates below, sometimes reaching depths of 200 to 300 feet. Meltwater from the snow and ice sometimes erodes the snow into the shape of an arch. These arches are not formed every year, but when they are they can be impressive; one was 40 feet high, 84 feet wide, and 255 feet long.

S

Snow's Brook, Mt.   approx. 3,000 feet   *Waterville Valley*

William Snow was an early settler of Waterville Valley who around 1830 built his cabin near this mountain.

Snyder Brook   *Northern Peaks*

In 1875 this brook draining the north side of Mt. Madison was named by the White Mountains trailmaker William G. Nowell, supposedly for the little dog of Charles E. Lowe, another trailmaker.

South Pond   *North Country*

South Pond, the site of a state park in Stark, was once the geographical counterpart of nearby North Pond, which has since been rechristened Christine Lake.

Spaulding Lake   *Great Gulf*

Located at the head of the Great Gulf, this tiny lake was named for John H. Spaulding, author of *Historical Relics of the White Mountains*, first published in 1855, and a manager of the Tip Top House on the summit of Mt. Washington. Spaulding was a hardy explorer of the White Mountains. In 1853 he first visited the lake later named for him, and in 1862 he made one of the earliest winter ascents of Mt. Washington. In 1891, on his seventieth birthday, he once again climbed Mt. Washington.

S

Spaulding's Tip Top House and the summit of Mt. Washington, from *Spaulding.*

Spaulding Spring   *Northern Peaks*

Near Edmands Col, between Mts. Jefferson and Adams, is a reliable spring discovered in 1875 by Rev. Henry G. Spaulding of Brookline, Massachusetts, and named for him by his companions Charles G. Lowe and W. G. Nowell.

Stairs, Mt.   3,460 feet   *Montalban Ridge*

Precipitous rock formations known as Giant Stairs are the origin of the name of this mountain on Montalban Ridge.

Stalbird Brook   *North Country*

In later life she was known to all in the town of Jefferson as Granny Stalbird, but when this hardy and determined woman first appeared in

White Mountains history she was Deborah Vickers, a young maiden working as a cook on the baronial estate of Col. Joseph Whipple. She lived in Jefferson eighteen months before she saw another white woman, and she is said to have made the first maple syrup in the fledgling settlement. She is also credited with bringing the first Bible to town; she paid five dollars for the Bible, the equivalent of ten weeks' wages on the Whipple estate.

Col. Whipple's reputation as a shrewd and parsimonious taskmaster has survived nearly 200 years. According to tradition, he once paid Deborah Vickers a year's wages in depreciated Continental currency, money he knew to be nearly valueless. When Deborah discovered she had been cheated, she confronted Col. Whipple when he returned from a trip to Portsmouth and so roundly and effectively upbraided him that he offered to give her any fifty acres in the town that had not already been sold, in addition to the payment she had already received. She had some of this land cleared before she temporarily left the White Mountains for Portsmouth, where she married Richard Stalbird. She returned to her homestead the next spring and exchanged some of her rocky land for better acreage. She remained in Jefferson the rest of her long life.

In the town of Shelburne a huge rock once stood that was known as Stalbird Ledge. The rock was destroyed during construction of a railroad line, but tradition has it that an aged woman named Stalbird once took refuge beneath the rock during a winter storm. The woman had to remain standing all night and until noon the next day, holding her horse's bridle. It's not certain the rock was named for Granny Stalbird of Jefferson, but the act would have been in character for her.

Stanton, Mt.   1,748 feet   *Montalban Ridge*

Probably named for a Bartlett family, this peak marks the beginning of Montalban Ridge. It was formerly known as Rattlesnake Mt., one of many mountains having that name in New Hampshire, but it appeared as Mt. Stanton on Prof. Charles Hitchcock's map of 1876.

Stark, Town   *North Country*

When it was first granted in 1774, this town on the Upper Ammonoosuc River was called Percy, named like its neighbor, Northumberland, for Hugh Smithson, Earl Percy and First Duke of Northumberland. It was renamed in 1832 for General John Stark, hero of the battles of Bunker Hill and Bennington, native son of New

Hampshire whose advice in a letter — "live free or die" — later became the state motto. The tiny settlement of Percy and the Percy Peaks in nearby Stratford retain the original name.

Starr King, Mt.   3,913 feet   *North Country*

The White Mountains have probably never had a more passionate and prolific popularizer than the Rev. Thomas Starr King. Born in 1824, he began visiting the region as a youth, and he later wrote about his explorations in the Boston *Transcript*. He became a Unitarian minister, and in 1859 his book *The White Hills: Their Legends, Landscapes, and Poetry*, was published. This book was very popular at the time, and in it he rhapsodized about the natural beauties of the White Mountains. He later moved to San Francisco, where he became an equally enthusiastic explorer of the mountains there, and a peak in Yosemite National Park is named for him. In the White Mountains, Mt. Starr King in the Pliny Range and King Ravine on Mt. Adams are reminders of him.

S

Stewartstown, Town   *North Country*

When Gov. John Wentworth first granted this town on the upper Connecticut River, he intended it to be developed by a group of men who included Sir George Colebrook and Sir James Cockburn, both connected with the British East India Company, and Sir John Stuart, Lord Bute, who had influence with the new king, George III. The group honored Lord Bute by naming their 6,000-acre holding Stuart. When the town was incorporated in 1799 after the Revolution, it was called Stewartstown, the name having reverted to the original Scottish form.

Stickney, Mt.   2,570 feet   *Zealand-Twin Mt.*

It's ironic that such an inconspicuous mountain as this should be named for the builder of such a magnificent edifice as the Mt. Washington Hotel. Joseph Stickney was a native of New Hampshire and for many years the owner of the Mt. Pleasant House. He built the Mt. Washington Hotel at Bretton Woods in 1901—02. Guests of the Mt. Pleasant House in 1878 called the mountain Ammonoosuc, but the name never came into general use.

Stinson Lake, Mt.   2,870 feet   *Moosilauke Region*

In April, 1752, a hunting party consisting of David Stinson of
Londonderry, Amos Eastman, and John Stark were attacked by Indians.
According to tradition, Stinson and Eastman were killed and scalped on
the shore of this lake near Rumney, while Stark was captured and taken
to Canada. He was later ransomed, and he went on to become a hero in
the Revolutionary War. The name Stinson Mt. first appeared on Philip
Carrigain's map of 1816.

Stratford, Town   *North Country*

If this town were named Stratford-on-Connecticut, the name would
be in keeping with its origins. Most if not all the Stratfords in the U. S. —
and they exist in Connecticut, New Jersey, Oklahoma, Texas, Virginia,
and Wisconsin — ultimately owe their names to Stratford-on-Avon,
home of William Shakespeare.

S

New Hampshire's Stratford was originally granted as Woodbury in
1762, named because many of its grantees came from Woodbury,
Connecticut. Totalling 48,063 acres, the grant was one of the largest ever
made in New Hampshire, but because of the Indian danger, few of the
grantees ever claimed their lands. In 1773 Gov. John Wentworth
regranted the land, this time under the name of Stratford, but the reason
was the same: many of the settlers were from Stratford, a town bordering
Woodbury in Connecticut.

Streeter Pond   *Franconia-Garfield*

Located south of Littleton, this pond was named for the first settlers
in its vicinity.

Success, Mt.   3,590 feet   *Mahoosuc Range*

This peak in the Mahoosuc Range takes its name from the town in
which it is located. The mountain has sometimes mistakenly been called
Mt. Ingalls, a name properly applied to a peak about two miles to the
south.

Success, Town   *Mahoosuc Range*

In the early 1770's, when relations between the colonies and England were worsening, some persons, such as Gov. John Wentworth, looked for signs of a more conciliatory attitude toward America. Thus, when word came in 1773 that the hated Stamp Act had been repealed, bells were rung, cannons were fired, and sermons were preached with the title "Good news from a far country." Gov. Wentworth was so elated by the news that he named an island on his Wolfeboro estate Stamp Act Island. Success was granted in 1773, and it is thought the name might have come from the Stamp Act repeal or the refusal of the colonists to allow British tea to be imported into Boston, a refusal many colonists viewed as a "success."

S   **Sugar Hill, Town**   *Cannon-Kinsman*

New Hampshire has forty-seven towns that were originally part of other towns, and Sugar Hill is the most recent. It was divorced from the town of Lisbon in 1962 after much litigation. Its name comes from a large grove of maple trees.

Sugarloaf Mt.   3,701 feet   *North Country*

The U. S. must have literally scores of mountains named Sugarloaf — all named because of their shapes. New Hampshire has at least five: one each in Benton, Stratford, Alexandria, and two in the Twin Mountain Range. Even Mt. Washington was named Sugarloaf for awhile. This peak in Stratford is the highest Sugarloaf in the White Mountains.

Surprise, Mt.   2,225 feet   *Carter-Moriah Range*

How this spur of Mt. Moriah got its name is obscure. A possible explanation is that the panoramic view from this minor peak does indeed come upon a hiker as a "surprise." The summit was cleared of trees in the mid-1800's by fire and wind. Another Mt. Surprise (947 feet) is located immediately east of Intervale.

Swazeytown *Waterville Valley*

In 1842 a man named Eben Swazey made a little clearing in Waterville Valley and settled there. And although Swazey left after ten years, the site has borne the name Swazeytown ever since — with one exception. Some loggers once had a camp and a dam there; they called the locality Crazytown.

Swift River *Conway-Bartlett-Jackson*

The Penacook name for this river paralleling the Kancamagus Highway was *chataguay*, meaning "the principal stream." The present name, clearly descriptive, appeared on Jeremy Belknap's map of 1791.

S

T

Tuckerman Ravine and Mt. Washington, from *King*.

T

Table Rock   *North Country*

No wider than a table — whence its name — this rock platform juts out from the north side of Mt. Gloriette in Dixville Notch and offers excellent views from its 700 foot height.

Tarleton Lake   *Moosilauke Region*

Col. William Tarleton, for whom this lake in Piermont was named, epitomized the patriotic enthusiasm that existed at the time of the Revolution. He fought in the Revolutionary War, was a delegate to the Constitution Convention of 1791, was a Presidential elector in 1804, and was a member of the New Hampshire Governor's Council in 1808. He had four sons, and he named them George Washington, Thomas Jefferson, Benjamin Franklin, and James Madison. Col. Tarleton settled on the lake later named for him, and he kept a tavern there.

Tecumseh, Mt.   4,004 feet   *Waterville Valley*

Numerous explanations exist as to how this peak came to bear the name of an Indian chief who lived hundreds of miles away. Tecumseh was a Shawnee chief (1768—1813) who joined his brother Tenskwatawa in an effort to unite the tribes of the Ohio region. The effort failed, through no fault of Tecumseh's, so he joined the British during the War of 1812 and was killed in the Battle of the Thames.

New Hampshire State Geologist Charles H. Hitchcock was once told that Mt. Tecumseh was named by E. J. Young, a Campton photographer whose stereos are the earliest photographs extant of Waterville Valley. Moses F. Sweetser, in his White Mountains guide, recorded as hearsay that the mountain was named by a Wisconsin tourist, who would have been more familiar with Chief Tecumseh. Nathaniel L. Goodrich, in his history of Waterville Valley, suggests

Terrace, Mt.

Michigan might have been meant instead of Wisconsin. He also suggests
that both Mts. Tecumseh and Osceola might have been named by E. J.
Connable of Jackson, Michigan, who came to Waterville Valley in 1859
and in 1863 built the present Patton cottage.

Terrace Mt.   3,670 feet   *North Country*

   This peak in the Pliny Range was named for its appearance from
the west.

Thompson and Meserve's Purchase   *Mt. Washington*

   In 1835, this 12,000-acre tract of land containing the north slope of
Mt. Washington and the summits of Mts. Adams, Jefferson, and Clay
was granted to Samuel W. Thompson of Conway and George P. Meserve
of Jackson. They paid $500 for their grant.

Thompson Falls   *Carter-Moriah Range*

   J. M. (Landlord) Thompson was the proprietor of the first Glen
House and laid out many paths in the area. He lost his life in the
Peabody River where the falls named for him are located.

Thoreau Falls   *Pemigewasset-Carrigain*

   Moses F. Sweetser in his White Mountains guide named these falls
on the North Fork of the Pemigewasset River for the famous writer and
naturalist Henry David Thoreau (1817—1862).

Thorn Mt.   2,287 feet   *Conway-Bartlett-Jackson*

   On Jeremy Belknap's map of 1791 this peak east of Jackson
appeared as Crotch Mt., but on Philip Carrigain's map of 1816 it
appeared under its present name. This name is thought to be derived
from the presence of thorn-bearing shrubs on the mountain.

Thornton, Town   *Pemigewasset-Carrigain*

Located on the Pemigewasset River, this town was founded as one of the earliest attempts to settle the wilderness using almost exclusively families from a single area. The grant was made in 1763 by Gov. Benning Wentworth, and most of the families were of Scots-Irish descent. They included Dr. Matthew Thornton (1714—1803), a Londonderry physician who at the age of four had come with his family from the Scots settlement in Londonderry, Ireland. Dr. Thornton was granted land in northern New Hampshire as a reward for having served as a surgeon in the Pepperell Expedition of 1745 during which New England troops captured Louisbourg, Nova Scotia. Dr. Thornton went on to become one of three persons from New Hampshire to sign the Declaration of Independence. He was also a justice of the New Hampshire Superior Court, a speaker in the House of Representatives, a member of the State Senate, a delegate to the Continental Congress, and first president — a position similar to governor — of New Hampshire following the Revolutionary War.

T

Three Sisters Ridge   *Chocorua Region*

The northeast ridge of Mt. Chocorua has three spurs only slightly lower than the summit, and from this comes the ridge's name.

Tin Mt.   2,025 feet   *Conway-Bartlett-Jackson*

The first discovery of tin in the U. S. was said to have been made on this low summit east of Jackson. Mining of the mineral followed its discovery, but active operations have long since ceased.

Tinker Brook   *North Country*
Samuel B. Robbins was a traveling tinker in the mid-1800's who went from house to house throughout northern New Hampshire. An eccentric character, he was overly fond of fishing in this brook near Berlin, and he chased away any local boys he found fishing there, much to their indignation and annoyance.

Tom, Mt.   4,047 feet   *Zealand-Twin Mt.*

In 1876 New Hampshire State Geologist Charles H. Hitchcock

named this peak west of Crawford Notch for Thomas J. Crawford, a son of Abel Crawford and for many years proprietor of the Crawford House.

Tripoli Road   *Waterville Valley*

Using an old logging railroad grade on its western side, this road through Thornton Notch was built by the U. S. Forest Service to connect Waterville Valley with Woodstock. It was completed in 1934, and the Forest Service assuaged fears of residents of Waterville Valley that a through route would end their seclusion by having the road bypass the town. The road owes its name to the Woodstock end of it having originally been opened for the Tripoli Mill in Thornton Gore. *Tripoli,* a diatomaceous mineral having numerous industrial uses, was dug from the bottom of East Pond.

T
Tripyramid, Mt.   4,110, 4,090, and 4,040 feet   *Waterville Valley*

Three distinct summits, nearly identical in height, are doubtless the origin of the name of this mountain east of Waterville Valley. The name was suggested by Prof. Arnold Guyot of Princeton, who in 1860 published a map of the White Mountains. The mountain had at one time been known as Passaconaway before that name was applied to another mountain.

Tuckerman Ravine   *Mt. Washington*

Dr. Edward Tuckerman (1817—1886) was a distinguished American botanist who for twenty years explored the White Mountains searching for botanical specimens. He first visited the White Mountains in 1837, staying with Abel Crawford, and later it was said of him that "no portion of the region, however dark its glens or inaccessible its peaks, was untrodden by his footsteps." This huge cirque on the south side of Mt. Washington was named for him as early as 1848, first appearing on a map in 1858.

Tumbledown-Dick Mt.   1,740 feet   *Mahoosuc Range*

According to tradition, a blind horse named Dick once "tumbled down" this steep cliff forming a spur of Bear Mt. north of Gilead, Maine.

Twin Mt.   4,926 and 4,769 feet   *Zealand-Twin Mt.*

Only about 150 feet of elevation separate these nearly identical peaks mid-way between Crawford and Franconia Notches. The higher summit is South Twin.

T

Mt. Washington and the Saco River, from *Drake.*

UV
WZ

UV
WZ

Umbagog, Lake   *North Country*

To the Abenaki Indians who once inhabited northern New Hampshire, the name of this lake straddling the New Hampshire—Maine border meant "clear lake" or "clear water." The name "Wambighe," which approximates the Abenaki pronunciation, appeared on a 1715 map of the region.

Valley Way   *Northern Peaks*

Conncecting the Appalachian trailhead on U. S. Rte. 2 with the Madison Hut, this path was built by the White Mountains trailmaker J. Rayner Edmands in 1895—97 using parts of paths cut previously by trailmakers L. M. Watson and E. B. Cook. It follows the valley of Snyder Brook, whence the name.

Vose Spur   *Pemigewasset-Carrigain*

This feature near Mt. Carrigain was named for Prof. G. L. Vose, who assisted in the New Hampshire Geological Survey conducted by Prof. Charles H. Hitchcock.

Wachipauka Pond   *Moosilauke Region*

In the mountains west of Glencliff is this pond, whose name in Abenaki meant "mountain pond." In Chatham is a pond whose name is also Mountain Pond, though there in English.

Walker Brook, Cascade, Ravine   *Franconia-Garfield*

The origin of the name of these features on the east side of Mt.

Lafayette is obscure. It might be noted that an A. S. Walker of Boston in July, 1855, climbed the old Glen Path to the summit of Mt. Washington *barefooted*, but it is unlikely that a connection exists between the names and the tough-soled hiker.

Wamsutta Trail   *Great Gulf*

This path leading from the Mt. Washington Auto Road to the Great Gulf Trail was named for the first of the six husbands of the Indian queen Weetamoo (see Six Husbands Trail).

Warren, Town   *Moosilauke Region*

W
The town of Warren, nestled in the hills south of Mt. Moosilauke, and Greenwich Village in New York City have one thing in common: a remarkable man named Peter Warren. Going to sea at fourteen, Peter by the time he was twenty-six was captain of his own ship, with seventy guns, and he continued to rise in position within the British Empire until he was eventually Sir Peter Warren, vice-admiral of the British Navy and Member of Parliament. The greatest achievement of his career, however, and the one that propelled him to greater fame, came in 1745 when he led a fleet of ships in the skillful capture of Louisbourg, Nova Scotia, a stronghold of the French, so strong it was called the "Dunkirk of America."Along the way in his career, Peter Warren married a sister of the governor of New York, and he invested some of the "prize money" from his sea conquests in land that is now Greenwich Village and Washington Square on Manhattan Island. But his name is probably better remembered in this town in the White Mountains, which he most likely never visited, The town was named for him when it was granted in 1764; Sir Peter Warren had died twelve years earlier.

Washington, Mt.   6,288 feet   *Mt. Washington*

The earliest names of this the highest peak in northeastern North America were simply descriptive. To the Abenaki-speaking peoples of the region, the peak was known as *Kodaak Wadjo*, meaning "summit of the highest mountain." It wasn't merely another peak to them, however, for they believed a *maji neowaska*, or "bad spirit," dwelt there. The Indians also called the peak *Agiochook*, which has been interpreted to mean "the place of the Great Spirit." To some tribes, the peak and its neighbors were called *Waumbekket-methna*, meaning "snowy mountains." And the Algonquin Indians called the peak *Waumbik*, meaning "white rocks."

A 1628 narrative refers to the mountain as the "Christall Hill," and Gov. Winthrop, writing in his journal in 1642 about Darby Field's ascent of the mountain that year, called the peak both "the White Hill" and "the Sugarloaf."

In 1784, a scientific party consisting of Dr. Manasseh Cutler, Dr. Jeremy Belknap, and several others climbed Mt. Washington as part of their explorations. Also in 1784, General George Washington, retired from the Army to Mt. Vernon, and the name Mt. Washington first appears in Dr. Cutler's manuscript reporting on the expedition. Later, Dr. Belknap used the name in the third volume of his *History of New Hampshire*, which appeared in 1792. This was the first appearance of the name in print.

The first known appearance of the name Mt. Washington on a map came five years later, when a map by the German mapmaker Sotzmann labeled the mountain "Washington B," the "B" standing for *berg*, which is German for "mountain."

Waternomee, Mt.   approx. 3,500 feet   *Moosilauke Region*

Formerly known as Blue Mt., this peak just south of Kinsman Notch became known under its present name in 1876 when the Appalachian Mountain Club approved the use of the name Waternomee. Waternomee was an Indian killed in the massacre led by Lt. Thomas Baker in the spring of 1712 at what later became known as Baker's River.

Waterville Valley, Town   *Waterville Valley*

By an act of the New Hampshire General Court in 1967, Waterville Valley became the official name of this tiny town surrounded by high peaks. The mountains — Tripyramid, Osceola, Tecumseh, Black, Sandwich, and Jennings — were once known as the Waterville Haystacks. The area was first settled in the 1760's, and the valley most likely took its name from its two rivers, the Mad and the Swift. The town was incorporated in 1829.

Watson Path   *Northern Peaks*

This path to the summit of Mt. Madison originally began at the

Ravine House in Randolph, but following the construction of other trails it now begins at Bruin Rock. The path is named for its maker, Laban M. Watson, who constructed it in 1882. The Watson family had been in Randolph since Laban's grandfather, Stephen Watson, bought a farm on the Moose River (he later drowned in the river). Stephen's son, Abel, continued the farm, as did Laban who turned it into the prosperous Ravine House, an important gathering place for trailmakers and hikers of the late 1800's. Watson guided and explored with William H. Peek, an association that lasted over twenty-five years. J. Rayner Edmands often joined them, and they would spend their days building trails and exploring and their nights at the Ravine House discussing their discoveries and making plans. Sometimes, when Eugene B. Cook was present, he would play his violin, and Chevalier Pychowska, a well known musician, would often enter into the merrymaking. It was one of the most important — and most delightful — eras of White Mountains history.

Waumbek, Mt.   4,020 feet   *North Country*

In some eastern Indian dialects, *waumbekket-methna* meant literally "snowy mountains," and in the Algonquin language *waumbik* meant "white rocks." From these comes the name of this peak in the Pliny Range in Randolph.

Webster, Mt.   3,910 feet   *Southern Peaks*

Topping the eastern bastion of Crawford Notch is this mountain, named as early as 1848 for the distinguished American statesman, lawyer, and native son of New Hampshire, Daniel Webster (1782—1852). Webster was no stranger to the White Mountains, and he praised them with his characteristic purple oratory. Yet he was also well familiar with the less pleasant aspects of the White Mountains. One sultry morning in June he set out to climb Mt. Washington with Ethan Allen Crawford as his guide. The weather was socked in by the time they reached the top, and when they arrived Webster delivered himself of the following address: "Mt. Washington, I have come a long distance and toiled hard to reach your summit. Now you seem to give me a cold reception, for which I am extremely sorry, as I shall not be able to view the grand prospect which now lies before me — and nothing prevents but the uncomfortable atmosphere in which you reside." As if in response, the mountain's "atmosphere" coated them with snow and sleet on their way down.

Weeks State Park, Mt.   3,890 feet   *North Country*

The Weeks family of Lancaster has had a long association with the White Mountains. The Rev. Joshua Wingate Weeks was one of the grantees of Lancaster in 1763, and roughly sixty years later John W. Weeks of Lancaster was one of the leaders of the party that ascended the Presidential Range and named most of the major peaks for U. S. Presidents. Still later, another John W. Weeks, who was Secretary of War during President Harding's administration, was instrumental in creating the White Mountain National Forest.

Secretary John Weeks built a mansion atop a hill south of the village of Lancaster, and it remained in family ownership until 1941 when John's children presented it to the State of New Hampshire as a memorial to their father. The state turned it into a state park, where the principal attraction is the mansion offering a commanding view of the upper Connecticut River valley and several mountain ranges. John's son, Sinclair Weeks, a U. S. Senator and Secretary of Commerce during President Eisenhower's administration, came from Washington to dedicate the state park to his father.

Mt. Weeks in the nearby Pilot Range was originally called Round Mt. because of its shape when viewed from the west, but now it too honors the Weeks family.

Weetamoo Fall, Trail, Mt.   2,548 feet *Great Gulf/Chocorua Region*

Weetamoo was an Indian *suncksqua*, or "queen," being the daughter of the great chief Passaconaway. According to tradition, she had six husbands at different times, whence the name of the Six Husbands Trail in the Great Gulf. Also in the Great Gulf is the Wamsutta Trail, named for the first of these husbands. Weetamoo Fall on the West Branch of the Peabody River in the Great Gulf is named for her, as is Weetamoo Mt. in the Sandwich Range and Weetamoo Trail, a southern approach to Mt. Chocorua.

Wentworth's Location   *North Country*

New Hampshire's colonial governors, the Wentworths, who granted so many thousands of acres to others and thus named them, set aside this tract of wild North Country land next to the Maine border for their own use. They never made much use of it, however, and it was not incorporated until 1881, when the original name was retained.

White Horse Ledge, from *Drake*.

White Horse Ledge   *Conway-Bartlett-Jackson*

W   On the west bank of the Saco River opposite North Conway is a cliff
much loved by rock climbers, on whose face is a light-colored patch that
some have said bears a resemblance to a dashing white horse. Legend has
it that unmarried women of the area who hoped to change their status
would look at the cliff, for an old New England tradition said that if a
maid or widow saw a white horse and then counted to one hundred, the
next man she saw would be her husband.

White Mountains

In all times, in all regions, people have called high mountains
"white." Dhaulagiri in the Himalayas, Craig Eyri in the Welsh
mountains, Mont Blanc in the Alps — all translate to mean "white
mountain." In northeastern North America, the Indians called Mt.
Washington *waumbekket-methna*, meaning "snowy or white
mountain." And some writers have said the high peaks of the
Presidential Range were also known as *kan-ran-vugarty*, a phrase
referring to their supposed resemblance to the whiteness of a gull.

The English mariner Christopher Levett is believed to have been
the first white man to have given the mountains a name. Writing in 1628
in his *A Voyage into New England*, Levett called one of them "the
Christall Hill," a name later writers attributed to quartz crystals being
found on peaks such as Mt. Washington. Darby Field found some of
these crystals when he ascended the mountain in 1642 — he thought they
were diamonds — but the name Crystal Hills was shortlived because it
was only thirty years later that the first mention of the name White

Mountains appeared in print. In 1672 John Josselyn in his *New England Rarities Discovered* wrote of the Indians: "Ask them whither they go when they die, they will tell you, pointing with their finger, to heaven beyond the White Mountains."

Josselyn also wrote in his account: "The original of all the great rivers in the countrie, the snow lies on the mountains the whole year excepting the month of August; the black flies are so numerous that a man cannot draw his breath but he will suck some of them in. Some suppose that the White Mountains were first raised by earthquakes, but they are hollow, as may be guessed by the resounding of the rain upon the level on the top."

Whiteface, Mt.   4,015 feet   *Chocorua Region*

In 1820 a great landslide laid bare one face of this mountain, and many persons have thought this to be the origin of the name. With little doubt, an exposed face of bedrock is indeed responsible for the name, but the 1820 slide was only one of many that have occurred on the mountain, for the name Whiteface was mentioned in Jeremy Belknap's journal of 1784, and it appears on Philip Carrigain's map of 1816, both preceding the 1820 slide.

Whitefield, Town   *North Country*

In 1774, Gov. John Wentworth granted this town on the Johns River north of Littleton; it was the last of the New Hampshire towns to be granted under English provincial rule. Although the name was originally listed as "Whitefields," the name was changed to the present spelling when the town was incorporated in 1804. The name honors George Whitefield, the English evangelist who was very popular at the time. He had toured New England and died at Exeter, New Hampshire, only four years before the granting of the town.

Wiggin Trail   *Chocorua Region*

In 1895 Thomas S. Wiggin cut this trail to connect the Dicey Mill Trail with the Blueberry Ledge Trail on Mt. Whiteface. The trail's nickname, "the Fire Escape," comes from the trail's steepness.

Wildcat Mt.   4,397 feet   *Carter-Moriah Range*

Now the site of a ski area, this peak on the east side of Pinkham Notch was called East Mt. on early maps. By 1860, when Prof. Arnold Guyot's map was published, it was called by its present name, which presumably was derived from the presence of wildcats on the mountain.

W

Crawford Notch, morning after the Willey Slide with Mt. Willard, background, from *Willey*.

Willard, Mt.   2,804 feet   *Zealand-Twin Mt.*

In 1844, Prof. Edward Tuckerman named this peak Mt. Tom in honor of Thomas Crawford, a White Mountains guide and proprietor of the Crawford House. But just a few years later Thomas Crawford himself renamed it, this time in honor of Joseph Willard of Boston, clerk of the Court of Common Pleas in Suffolk County. Willard was a guest at the Mt. Crawford House, and together with Thomas Crawford he climbed the mountain named for him.

Willard Basin, Notch   *North Country*

According to local tradition, a man named Jonathan Willard came to the North Country from southern New Hampshire and became an eccentric recluse in the area later named for him. He was supposed to have been a cousin of Gov. Henry Hubbard, but he was content to live alone in the wilderness with only his dog Pilot for companionship.

When the old hermit became infirm, his son came and took him back to civilization whence he had fled. Local tradition also has it that nearby Pilot Mt. was named for Willard's dog, but in fact, records show that the name predates the hermit, and that may also be true for Willard Notch and Basin, for these names appear on maps as early as 1816.

Willey, Mt.   4,302 feet   *Zealand-Twin Mt.*

In June, 1826, members of the Samuel Willey family looked out from their home in Crawford Notch toward this mountain and witnessed a landslide that greatly frightened them. They thought, however, that such a slide was unlikely to occur again. They were tragically wrong.

Two months later, following heavy rains, a massive amount of earth, rocks, and trees descended from the mountain and wiped out the entire family. They undoubtedly sensed a slide was impending, for they fled their house, and most authorities believe they ran towards shelter in an outlying root cellar. They would have done better to have remained in the house, for a boulder behind the house caused the avalanche to split, and following the slide the house was the only building left standing.

The heavy rains caused severe flooding throughout the area, and soon friends and neighbors of the Willeys became concerned for their safety. A party that included Ethan Allen Crawford arrived at the Willey homestead and found the family's cattle unmilked while all about lay ruin and destruction. Searching amidst the rubble they found the bodies of Mr. and Mrs. Willey, two hired men, and two of the Willey's daughters. The bodies of three other children — one daughter and two sons — were never found. Ethan Allen Crawford later told his wife Lucy that he wept openly at the scene, only the second time tears had come to his eyes since he had achieved manhood.

Prof. Edward Tuckerman ascended the mountain in 1845, and he named the mountain for the family it had destroyed.

Wonalancet Village, Mt.   2,800 feet   *Waterville Valley*

Wonalancet, whose name means "governor," was a great Indian chief, the son and successor of the chief Passaconaway. Wonalancet ruled his people from 1660 to 1685, and during this time he sought to maintain peaceful relations with his white neighbors, even during King Philip's War. His attempts to restrain his people ultimately failed, however, and defeated and dejected he resigned his chieftancy.

The name for this mountain was suggested by the poet Lucy

Larcom, a protege of John Greenleaf Whittier and like him a great enthusiast of the White Mountains. Wonalancet Village was originally called Birch Intervale, but in 1893 its name was changed to honor the chief. The mountain was formerly known as Toadback.

Woodstock, Town   *Pemigewasset-Carrigain*

The present name of this town on the Pemigewasset River is the third official name it has had during its history. When it was first granted in 1763 to Eli DeMerritt by Gov. Benning Wentworth it was called Peeling. The most likely origin of this name is that it came from an English town of that name. But because the grant consisted of sections pared off from surrounding towns, an apocryphal story says that DeMerritt named it because, "As this grant seems to be the peelings of all creation, let us call the township Peeling."

W   DeMerritt didn't settle in Peeling, and the lands were later regranted. In 1771, Gov. John Wentworth renamed the town Fairfield, after Fairfield, Connecticut. But again settlement of the lands lagged, and the original name of Peeling persisted. This was not without opposition, however, and in 1813 a Rev. Benjamin Ropes preached a sermon — lasting until three o'clock in the afternoon — on the inappropriateness of the name Peeling. There was no reference in the Bible for it, he said; no town could prosper with such a name, and he urged the town's inhabitants to "peel it off."

Finally, in 1840, the name was changed again, this time to Woodstock, a name taken by many New England towns. It comes from the site of a historic palace in England that was also the setting for Sir Walter Scott's novel *Woodstock*.

Woodsville, Village   *Connecticut Region*

Wood was responsible for the name of this town on the confluence of the Connecticut and Ammonoosuc Rivers, but not in the manner one might think. In 1830 a man named John L. Woods came from nearby Wells River, Vermont, to build a sawmill on the Ammonoosuc River, and from this beginning Woods prospered, eventually helping to make the town named for him the second most important railroad center in the state (Concord was the first). The village was originally called Governor's Farm or Governor's Reservation, because the Wentworths, in granting land, customarily reserved 500 acres for themselves to be assured of a future say in local government. All such lands were eventually returned to the towns.

Zealand Notch, Mt.   4,301 feet   *Zealand-Twin Mt.*

The origin of this name is obscure, but it appeared on early maps and records as New Zealand, suggesting some association with the islands in the South Pacific. The area was once described as the most beautiful virgin forest in the White Mountains, but soon after it was destroyed by fire. The virgin timber also attracted the nineteenth century lumber baron James Everett Henry, and upon his logging operations grew a thriving community, complete with boardinghouses, a church, a school, a post office, a mill, and two train stations that at one time received as many as five trains a day to transport logs. Fire continued to plague the area, however, striking in 1886, 1897, and finally in 1903, the last fire destroying 84,000 acres of timber.

Henry knew the monetary value of White Mountains scenery, and when the Mt. Washington House was being built, featuring a view of a beautiful maple-covered hillside that Henry owned, he informed the hotel's owners that unless they purchased the hillside from him at an inflated price he would log it and turn its trees into charcoal. The hotel people tried calling his bluff, but when Henry's crews began cutting and burning the trees they capitulated. Henry loved telling the story of his squeeze-play, the price he received growing with each telling.

BIBLIOGRAPHY

Albany, New Hampshire, 1766-1966, Bicentennial Observance, 1966.

Anderson, John, and Morse, Stearns, *The Book of the White Mountains,* New York, 1930.

Appalachian Mountain Club, *The A.M.C. White Mountain Guide,* Boston, 1907—1979.

Beals, Charles Edwards, Jr., *Passaconaway in the White Mountains,* Boston, 1916.

Belknap, Jeremy, *History of New Hampshire* (3 vols.), Boston and Philadelphia, 1784—1792, reprint, Hampton, N. H. , 1973.

_____ ,"A New Map of New Hampshire," *History of New Hampshire, vol. 2,* Boston, 1791.

Bent, Allen H., "The Indians and the Mountains," *Appalachia,* June, 1915, pp. 257—271.

_____, *A Bibliography of the White Mountains,* Boston, 1911, reprint, E. J. Hanrahan, ed., Somersworth, N. H., 1971.

Berlin, Historical Committee, *Berlin New Hampshire Centennial,* 1829—1929, Berlin, N. H., 1929.

Blanchard, Col., and Rev. Mr. Langdon, Geographer of His Majesty, *An Accurate Map of His Majesty's Province of New Hampshire in New England,* Portsmouth, N. H., 1761.

Bond, George P., *A Map of the White Mountains,* 1853.

Bowles, Ella Shannon, *Let Me Show You New Hampshire,* New York, 1938.

Bryant, W. C., ed., *Picturesque America,* Part Seven, New York, 1872.

Burt, Frank H., "The Nomenclature of the White Mountains," *Appalachia,* Dec., 1915, pp. 359—390.

_____ , "The Nomenclature of the White Mountains II," *Appalachia*, June, 1918, pp. 261—268.

_____ , "The White Mountains Forty Years Ago," *Appalachia*, Dec., 1916, pp. 37—49.

Carrigain, Philip, *A Map of New Hampshire*, Concord, N. H., 1816.

Child, Hamilton, comp., *Grafton County Gazeteer, 1709—1886*, Syracuse, N. Y., 1886.

Choate, Malcolm C., Underhill, Miriam, and Underhill, Robert L. M. , *Kearsarge: on the History of the Name as Applied to the Mountain in Carroll County, N. H.*, report to the Appalachian Mountain Club, 1957.

Conrad, Justus, *The Town of Woodstock and Its Scenic Beauties*, Littleton, N. H.

Crawford, Lucy, *Lucy Crawford's History of the White Mountains*, edited by Stearns Morse, Hanover, N.H., 1966. (First edition: *White Hills*, 1846.)

Cross, George N., *Randolph Old and New: Its Ways and Its By-Ways*, Town of Randolph, N. H., 1924.

_____ , "Randolph Yesterdays," *Appalachia*, Dec., 1916, pp. 49—58.

Cutter, Louis F., "The Edmands Paths and Their Builder," *Appalachia*, Aug., 1921, pp. 134—140.

Drake, Samuel Adams, *The Heart of the White Mountains*, New York, 1882.

Dummer Bicentennital Committee, *History of Dummer, New Hampshire, 1773—1973*, Littleton, N. H., 1973.

Eastman, Samuel C., *The White Mountain Guide Book*, Concord, N.H., 1858—1884.

Evans, George Hill, *Handbook of Cold River Valley and Adjacent Territory*, Chatham Trails Assoc., Chatham, N. H., 1932.

Farmer, John, and Moore, Jacob B., *A Gazeteer of the State of New-Hampshire*, Concord, N. H., 1823.

Fay, Charles E., "The Annual Address of the President: Our Geographical Nomenclature," *Appalachia*, June 1882, pp. 1—3.

Goodrich, Nathaniel L., *The Waterville Valley: A Story of a Resort in the New Hampshire Mountains*, Lunenburg, Vt., 1952.

Gore, Effie K., and Speare, Eva A., comps., *New Hampshire Folk Tales*, New Hampshire Federation of Women's Clubs, 1932, revised, Littleton, N. H., 1964.

Hammond, Otis G., *A Checklist of New Hampshire History*, Concord, N. H., 1925, reprint, E. J. Hanrahan, ed., Somersworth, N. H., 1971.

Hart, Warren W., "Timothy Nash," *Appalachia*, June, 1919, pp. 383—390.

Hitchcock, Charles H., "Map of New Hampshire," atlas accompanying *Report on the Geology of New Hampshire*, New York, 1878.

Holland, Samuel, *A Topographical Map of the State of New Hampshire*, London, 1784.

Horne, Ruth B. D., *Conway Through the Years and Whither*, Conway, N. H., 1963.

Horton, Louise S., Underhill, Elizabeth H., and Deal, Eleanor D., *Piermont, New Hampshire (1764—1947)*, Bradford, Vt.

Huden, John C., *Indian Place Names of New England*, New York, 1962.

Hunt, Elmer Munson, *New Hampshire Town Names and Whence They Came*, Peterborough, N. H., 1970.

_____ , "The Origin of Some New Hampshire Mountain Names," *Historical New Hampshire*, April, 1955, pp. 1—28.

Joy, Thelma, and Georgia, Ann, eds., *Woodstock, New Hampshire, Celebrates 200 Years*, North Woodstock, N.H.

Kilbourne, Frederick W., *Chronicles of the White Mountains*, Boston, 1916.

King, Thomas Starr, *The White Hills: Their Legends, Landscape, and Poetry*, Boston, 1859.

Leavitt, Franklin, *A Map of the White Mountains*, Boston, 1852.

Lehr, Frederic B., *Carroll, New Hampshire: The First 200 Years, 1772—1972*, Littleton, 1972.

Lewis, Samuel, *Map of the State of New Hampshire*, Philadelphia, 1794.

—————— , *Arrowsmith and Lewis New and Elegant General Atlas* 1805.

Merrill, Georgia Drew, *History of Carroll County*, Boston, 1889, reprint, Somersworth, N. H., 1971.

—————— , *History of Coos County, New Hampshire*, Boston, 1888, reprint, Somersworth, N. H., 1972.

Milan Bicentennial History Committee, *Historical Notes and Pictures of Milan, New Hampshire, 1771—1971*, Littleton, 1971.

New Hampshire, A Guide to the Granite State, Federal Writers' Project, Works Progress Administration, Boston, 1938.

Nilsen, Kim R., *A History of Whitefield, New Hampshire, 1774—1974*, Whitefield, N. H., 1974.

Oakes, William, *Scenery of the White Mountains*, Boston, 1848.

O'Kane, Walter Collins, *Trails and Summits of the White Mountains*, Boston, 1925.

Olsen, John, "Pinkham Woods," *Appalachia*, Dec., 1946, pp. 225—230.

Peabody, Dean, Jr., "The Evolution of the AMC Hut," *Appalachia*, Dec., 1931, pp. 432—437.

Poole, Ernest, *The Great White Hills of New Hampshire*, New York, 1946.

Powers, Rev. Grant, *Historical Sketches of the Discovery, Settlement, and Progress of Events in the Coos Country and Vicinity, Principally Included Between the Years 1754 and 1785*, Haverhill, N. H., 1841, reprint, 1880.

Proctor, Mary A., *The Indians of the Winnepesaukee and Pemigewasset Valleys*, Franklin, N. H., 1930.

Randall, Peter, *Mount Washington: A Guide and Short History*, Hanover, N. H., 1974.

Slosson, Annie Trumbull, *Fishin' Jimmy*, New York, 1889.

Spaulding, John H., *Historical Relics of the White Mountains*, Boston, 1855.

Stark Bicentennial Committee, *History of Stark, New Hampshire, 1774—1974*, Littleton, 1974.

State Papers, *N. H. Town Charters, vols, I—II*, Albert Stillman Batchellor, ed., Concord, N. H., 1895.

Swan, Bradford F., "The Earliest Map of the White Mountains," *Appalachia*, 1964—65, pp. 386—388.

Sweetser, M. F., *The White Mountains, A Handbook for Travellers*, Boston, 1876.

Thompson, Jeanette R., *History of the Town of Stratford, New Hampshire, 1773—1925*, Concord, N. H., 1925.

Tuckerman, Frederick, "Early Visits to the White Mountains," *Appalachia*, Aug., 1921, pp. 111—127.

Upham, Warren, "Unnamed Mountains Between Mt. Hancock and Scar Ridge," *Appalachia*, Feb., 1878, pp. 252—258.

Wight, Denman B., *The Androscoggin River Valley: Gateway to the White Mountains*, Rutland, Vt., 1967.

Willey, Benjamin G., *Incidents in White Mountain History*, Boston, 1856.

Woodbury, Elmer E., *Historical Narrative of "Lost River" and "Kinsman Notch,"* Littleton, N. H., n.d.

INDEX

Names in parentheses indicate former or secondary present names. Names in quotes are primarily Indian names.